Never
Understand Me

My ghetto qur'an

S a h e e m   W r i g h t

iUniverse, Inc.
Bloomington

Never Understand Me
My ghetto qur'an

iUniverse books may be ordered through booksellers or by contacting:

iUniverse
1663 Liberty Drive
Bloomington, IN 47403
www.iuniverse.com
1-800-Authors (1-800-288-4677)

ISBN: 978-1-4620-1780-5 (sc)
ISBN: 978-1-4620-1781-2 (e)

Printed in the United States of America

iUniverse rev. date: 07/28/2011

Contents

Part 1

Prologue   vii

Never Understand Me   1

Black Rain   23

These Days   45

Epilogue   89

Part 2

Love Is Black   91

Soul &Heart   133

My "Ghetto Quran"   175

The Lost Poems Of E.X. My Father   183

Love Notes & Pictures   209

Prologue

No worry (So Sorry) Pt. 1 Dedicated to: Mama & Daddy

What's wrong mama stop crying, I'm only going away. It's not like I'm dying, 5 months in this bitch! But I maxed out. Fucking crackers always try to put a nigga out. Why, why, why couldn't that little bitch just lie? Why, why, why? I should've hit that little bitch in the eye. It's all good; I'm back in the hood nothing changes. The same shit, some nigga's strange everybody and they pops trying to get a little change. Niggas is so phony even family will do you in. The ones you thought you knew never really knew you. It's a fucked thing to say but it's true. Then if it isn't worse I came back to this shit. Now I'm thinking on ways to get myself bent, smoking blunts every day. To ease the stress fuck these hoe's I won't deal with the mess. I'm too sharp to shift; I know this for a fact jack. When these hoes try to run game on me I just spit it right back now this nigga in the club fighting over his hoe. Nigga fuck that hoe give me the dough; Or something bigger than money you can't even spin. Then I'm going to Bend out the country (fuck it). One of these days I will find a down ass bitch that's on my level, and give me 110 % of everything that's yours. Your soul too, let my pops holler at your mom's so we can keep it all in the family.

Don't start saying three months down the line you can't stand me. It's all good nigga I'm still riding with you thru your little 10 year bid, but I got to do what I got to do. If I got it you got it. Nothing changes. If I don't see you till I'm 30 Years old it's all good. I should be filthy fucking rich .Mama you broke my heart when u chose that nigga over your #1st born flesh and blood son. But I still love you. I still do, but I'm going to end the passage by keep the faith never stop praying.

"Dear mama I'm a man now" I want to make it on my own, Not a hand out.

"My ghetto Life story" "Too Gangsta for anything"

Never Understand Me

another one

    for those Wondering.

    Mr Ex

and you think its thru I
am But one person I Thought
you knew, you must really dont
know me, you say you got money
dont even show me, cause I got
kids to feed and looking for a Jack,
~~SKIP~~ mothafussing Black thats talking
smack, still selling CRACK, ~~dude~~ u
small time, grow some nots B a
man, I dont wants hear that this
and that I do what I can,
I cant stand that, as I mater
of fact I cant stand ~~you~~, Nigga
Im still getting money and gckng
funny now, ~~dude~~ every Body
I want out.

Another One

(For those wonder Mr. Ex)

An you think it's thru I am but one person. I thought you knew,
You must really don't know me; you say you get money,
Don't even show me because I got kids to Feed and looking for a jack.
Skip mother fussing black that's talking smack, still
Selling crack, Dude you small time grow some nuts and be a man.
I don't want to hear this and that I do what I can,
I can't stand that. Matter of fact I can't stand
You. Nigga I'm still getting money and acting funny
Now fuck everyone I want out.

BROKEN
home pt.1
2 mama & daddy

I'm Just sitting hear drinking a
Bottle of Kessler thinking aBout my
Childhood what was good and what was
Fucked up. half my Life I was Ruffed
up. People Lied and stole From me if
they could of got my sole they would of
sole From me It was crazy and my
mama she was Lazy But she Ketp the
Famliy together, (Kind of) was a crack
Fen mama still a Black queen mama
what Did I do so Bad Dat made you
mad that you Beat me even tryed too
Cbeat me and why? Cause I Look Like
my Father? Lord knows so much Bullshitt
only gotting harder and my Father thats
a hole diffent story these nigga's got
me Fucked up I'm Beggin For glory
Its a shame is you still my man or did
you walk out? Went to Prison oh shit
put the chalk out But too make a
Short Story Breif mama, Daddy hold
my hand stay neif.

                Love y'all,
                        Lil Earl

        "abdul Raheem"

            peace

-4-

Broken Home Part 1

4 mama & daddy

I'm just sitting hear drinking bottle of Kessler thinking about my child hood
What was good and what was fucked up. Half my life I was ruffed up.
People lied and stole from me if they could have got my soul
They would have stolen from me. It was crazy and mama, she was lazy
But she kept the family together (kind of). Was a crack Fein mama,
Still a black Queen Mama… What did I do so bad that made you mad at me?
That you beat me even tried to cheat me why? Cause I look like my father?
Lord knows so much bullshit only had gotten harder and my father
That's a whole different story. These niggas got me fucked up.
I'm begging for glory. It's a shame are you still my man or did u walk out?
Went to prison, oh shit put the chalk out but too make a long story brief
Mama, daddy holds my hand stay near?   Love y'all Abdul Raheem peace

1996.

Never Understand me
pt.1

Its like they Just Dont understand, I'm only
FIFTEEN an still tryna Be a man, my plan one day
is to Be Rich a Poverty, tell me why I gotta get
stuck in this? mayBe its my Roots, Just where
I Come From you know. They SAY I'm CRazy
Cause I REFuse to Let go, I think about
my past an my Life right Now, my mother dOing
Crack and my Father Locked Down. what a Ugly
picture! Again, I'm only FIFteen with a Gin Bottle in
my hand, I wANt to Kill my self Just to see
were I Stand.

poverty   Cry for help

This is:
The Very first
poem I wrote
When I was fifththteen

REAdy 2 dyE

Never Understand Me

part 1

It's like they just don't understand, I'm only fifteen
I'm still trying to be a man. My plan One day is to be rich.
Poverty tell me why I got to get stuck like this? Maybe it's my Roots
Just where I come from you know they say I'm crazy because I refuse to let go.
I think about my past and my life right now my mother doing crack
Father locked down what an ugly picture! Again I'm only fifteen
With a gin bottle in hand I want to kill myself
Just to see where I stand.
Cry for help

(1st poem written 1996 fifteen yrs. old)

young man   young Woman

I Love you For who you are.
I Love you For Being yourself.
I Love you Because your Love
have given me good health.
I know WE'Ve had are problems and
I wish I could take them Back
But the Fact remains WE are
still here still together thru
all the Bad Weather. I still Love
you, try Not 2 Put Knowone above
you. you are the mother of my
Kids and I Love are Family.
Sometimes When I down you
Bring me sanaitiy.

M.E

A
R
L

A
r
l
e
t
a

King & Queen.

Young man, young women

I love you for who you are (even if you don't know).
I love you for being yourself. I love you because your love has given good health.
 I know we've had our problems and I wish I could take them back,
But the fact remains we are still here still together thru all the bad weather.
I still love you. You are the mother of my kids and I love our family.
Sometimes when I'm down you bring me sanity.

M.E.

Young People

Be easy homey slow down stop
moving so fast take yo time
make it last. Cause it could
end in a minute and Before
you know it you up in it,
a casket, and Now N says
they dont share tear drops
They just close the thing.
Anther young Dude gone off
the amercian dream, If children
is truely the furture we is in
Some trouble somebody call the
Roit police on the Double, an
if you dont you; throught you had
Prolbems Before; shit is about to
get worse. Somebody anyBody Needs
to teach are children I mean
are Babys; Dudes stop making
Babys and Running, I mean Really.
Females stop acting silly yall are
the mothers the carriers without
yall it cant Be us. The way things
is going in this time in age I
Just grow with Decise.

damn!!

Young People

Be easy homey slow down stop moving so fast take your time make it last,

Because it could end in a minute and before you know it you up in it.

A casket and now in days they don't shed tear drops they
 Just close the damn thing.

Yet another young dude has gone off the American dream.

If children are truly our future we is in some trouble somebody call the riot
police on the double.

And if you thought you had problems before shit about to get worse someone
needs to
Teach your children I mean babies.

Dude stop making baby's and running I mean really females stop acting
silly you all
are the mothers the carriers without you all there is no us.

The way things are going in this time in age I just grow with lust.

March 14

So Beautiful
                (Raheem)

When I First saw you I cryed
Like A BaBy inside. God Bless me
again. it was magical. I would
Not trade that feeling For Nothing
in the world , you mama through
you was a girl But I knew
you Was my son. Second Born;
But still Number one, I know
you gonna make me proud, I
Wish yo sister could see you
~~~~~ Cant wait till you get
Odder, and watch all the People
trya Be you. I see you.
I watch you when you
sleep you Look so peace
Full ~~~ Sound Like a herd of
Sheep. Ima trya Be around As
Long as I can For you, to
watch you grow into a man.
an in dew time you'll truely
Understand, everything.

                        Love you
                        Lil Homey.

- 12 -

So beautiful

(4 my son Raheem the prince)march14th

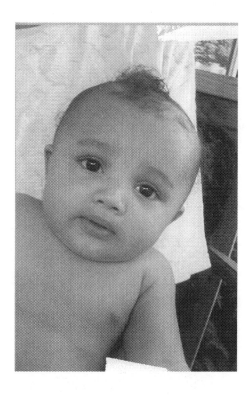

When I first say you I cried like a like a baby inside,
God has blessed me again It was magical
I would not trade that feeling for nothing in the world
Your mama thought you was a girl but I knew you were my son #2 bad boy
But still my number one I know you going to make me proud
I wish your sister could see you now can't wait till you get older
And watch all the people try to be you.
I watch you when you sleep look so peaceful sound like a herd of sheep.
I'm trying to be around as long as I can for you and your brother
To watch yawl grow into men an in due time Yawl truly will understand
everything. Love you little homey

BE FREE

To Be Free I mean truely Free
Free From all the Stress, niecative
Foney ness, iknow more of that please
A Need a release, Let me Breath
But I anit gonna 'smoke know weed
How can I acieive my
Girl compain again & again. why
Should I have to deal with it?
I would rather Be a playa, Deal
with it.

Be Free

To be free I mean truly free. Free from all the stress

And negative phony mess. Know more of that please

I need release to let me breath but I will not smoke a weed.

How can I achieve? My girl complains again and again.

Why should I have to deal with it I would rather be a playa

Deal with it!

What I'm like

A man being murdered same time a baby is born the beginning and end.
As far as poetry it's only natural that I describe my name of the essence
That defines my name. First it was lil earl but times have changed ask me
now I'm the artist for what I write might sound plain Took my time in the game
kept my mind off the fame saw fiends shoot up in do lines of cocaine saw my
close friend killed it almost tore me apart it
Hurt my heart like Martin Luther shot in the dark know more of that
Please I beg for mercy but who has cursed me I'm just thirsty for justice
I mean knowledge it's just us. I'm just trying to send my kids to college
When will I see the day that we can prevail how much money's enough
Without going to jail?

So VICIOUS

I still Lie,

Dont ask me why, I Just Do, telling these girls I Love them, in this telling me what they will do, good game coming from that MAN who got it all baby give ME your number an I will Call, dont even trip, you wanta ball? I probuly by you a fit at the mall, if you looking Bomby Broke talking Boot you aint got know money, I will Front ya But if you keep Pulling that I might have to Jump ya

Cause Im Not yo sugar, Daddy, Just Because you see me in that old School caddy whit Them Suave Ballys on my Feet you think its Sweet, you look at mee an Say damn!, I look at you an say Flesh Meat, ~~Devore~~ Its Like this, I treat them how I meet them, I tell you what you want & hear, thats I greet them, Im more than a man, more then your friend; till the end this how we blend, let us bl...

Do what we do, you still telling me what you want Do but I know you bout too, I doubt you never met a dude like me, I do you Im one of kind there is only one me, so if you still don't know, I, Doubt you will find out, so why don't you get yo game up an show me what you about.

Lile tha Dead

So vicious

(I still lie)

Don't ask me why I do. Telling these girls I love them and they tell me what
they will do.
Good game coming from the man that has it all baby give your number
And I will call don't even trip you want to ball? I might buy you a fit at the
mall if you're looking bomb.
Broke Talking about you don't have no money I will front cha, but you keep
pulling that I might have to jump cha.
Cause I'm not your sugar daddy. Just because you see in that old school
Caddy with suave shoes on my feet you think it's sweet.
You look at me and say damn I look at you and say fresh meat.
It's like this I treat them like I meet them I tell them what they want to hear
That's how I greet them I'm more than a man more than friend till the end
This is how we bend let us blend.
Do what we do you still telling me what you won't do but you about too
I doubt you never met a dude like me I told you I'm one of kind
There is only one e so if you still don't know
I doubt you'll find out so step your game up and show me what your about.

2001

Never Understood me
part 2   By Lil Earl

They never understood me but its 5 five
years later and im still Laughing
See you Look deep in my soul
an I'm really crying or maybe dying
I ask myself why, is this Life
Was I meant 4 this me? Why must I
Fall victim to a cruel World and my
Girl say only time will tell but how
much Longer do I have to wait
Till its to Late, but I truly believe
once I cross that Gate I will be
straight.
                    E

Never understand me

part 2

They never understand me but its five years later and

I'm still laughing see you Look deep in my soul an really

I'm crying or maybe dying I ask myself why, is this

Life was this meant for me why I must fall victim to a cruel world

My girl say only time will tell but how much longer do I

Have to wait till it's too late but I truly

Believe once I cross that gate I will be straight. E

Black Rain

Black rain
(how it is)

So it falls from the sky from the top or above, streadin so much rain 2 the gain of evil, we all pray that one day it will end, but at the same time we all sin, Sell yo sole 4 gold, money, jewerly, & cars, & spend a life time of imprisonment behind bars, its a shame we represent 37% of the country, an have of that is ether dead or locked up, but know body wants 2 b locked up, I guess its just yo nature, Stress gettin major, wanta smoke a square every minute, Thinken life; why is Ihm in it+?, Try 2 stay focus wit my mind on fame, but that Black rain brings haters in the game, "hate" another strong word, from 400 years 2 flippin the bird my nerve still tinchin, niggas itchin 4 a stretch, Had 2 fall back 2 recop, stop sellin rocks cause it aint making no money, plus my girl tum bout "she tired of that 'honey', its kinda funny an game, but thats what y get outta Black rain.

from the writing of Abdul Rahim
"peace be with you"

Black rain

(how it is)

So it falls from the sky from the top or above spreading so much rain to gain
of evil.
We all pray that one day it will end but at the same time we all sin.
Sell your soul for gold, money jewelry and cars spend a life time of
Imprisonment behind bars it's a shame we represent 37% of the country,
An half of that population is either dead or locked up.
Nobody wants to be locked up; I guess it's just your nature stress getting major
Want to smoke a square every minute thinking life why is I'm in it?
Trying to stay focused with my mind off fame but this black rain
Brings haters in the game. Hate another strong word from 400 years.
To flipping the bird. My nerves still itching nigga twitching 4 a scratch.
Had to fall back to recap stop selling rocks cause it isn't making no money
Plus my girl talking bout I'm tired of that honey! It's kind of funny.
And somewhat lame but that's what you get out of black rain.

-Abdul Raheem

I cry
to 2 mama

I Cry, But not the way my tears can show, I cry, only when my anger Lets go, Sometimes I Look at things and I wonder why? Why Cry, So much pain was Inflicted through my child hood youth, till this day I still dont Know the truth, Well maybe I do and Just cant forget it, It hurt so much I just cant admit it, Why? Why did my Grandmother have 2 die? She never did nothing 2 Nobody, why, why did my mother have 2 Lie? I thought she really Loved me. Life sometimes Can take u threw trips, one minute u on top Kickin it the next u slip. Its kind of Funny how things Can turn out I'm over here u over there. Just how every thing went about, I never stole from u why did u Steal from me? We use to B so Close Now its Life my health, my heart is so empty. Allah Said Love thou mother & I always will, But I will Never Forget what we went threw, Something a mother & a son Shoudne Been threw. I pray & I hope we can Finlay Come 2 Kiss, make something we once had Co-exiss!

                from the writings of Abdul Rahim
                "peace be with you"

I cry

(dedicated to mama)

I cry but not the way my tears can show I cry only when my anger lets go
Sometimes I look and think and I wonder why, why cry?
So much pain was inflicted thru my childhood youth till this day
I still don't know the truth. Well maybe I do and just can't forget it,
It hurts so much I just can't admit it why?
Why did grandmother have to die she never did nothing to nobody
Why, why, why did mother have to lie? I thought she really loved me
Life can sometimes take u thru trips one minute you on top kicking it the next u slip.
Its kina funny how things can turn out I'm over here and you're over there.
Just how everything went about. I never stole from you why did u steal from me
We used to be so close now it like my heart my heart is so empty.
Allah said love thy mother and I always will
But I will never forget what we went thru Some things a mother and son should
have never been thru. I pray and I hope we can finally come 2 kiss
make something we once had coexist-
Peace be with you-Abdul Raheem

"Cold"

Little poet

From a harsh reality 2 escapin, Fate, I wonder, will I smile on Judgment day?, Will it b bright or will it b dark?, me & my people have suffered so long, that we have Fall apart, I have spent alot of Cold days an lonely nights wanderen threw time, thinkin, that I may recive from this great depression, my obsession 4 girls & money is greatly mixed, 4 this, is my weakness on with I can be beatin, The Choices that I make are greatly mistreatin, I walk around actin a clown lookin so me, hangin with the homeboys Just 2 b a "G", Its Kinda Lame, but its a shame niggas cant Learnt, dont get Burnt Buy the same girl twice, aint nothing nice, put yo ass on Ice, 4 a minute, represent, but recounize, where yo fuckin sense at, If y dont understand shit, understand this, aint no hope 4 the Future 4 Black people in this Country, why we hungry an still beggin 4 Change?, "Change", a strange word in the lives of many, Nr a penney Low 2 SUSSESS, and we Still Strewed in the game, and its a shame how Black kids Can have So much vain, & pain.

from the writings of Abdul Rahim
"peace be with you"

Cold

From a harsh reality 2 escaping fate I wonder will I smile on judgment day.
Will it be bright or will it be dark? My people and I have suffered so
Long that we have fallen apart I have spent a lot of cold days and lonely nights
Wondering thru time thinking that I may recline from this great depression
My obsession 4 girls and money are greatly missed
4 this is my weakness on which it can be beating,
The choices that I make are greatly mistreated.
I walk around acting a clown looking so me hanging with homeboys
Just to be a g it's kind of lame but it's a shame niggas have not learned
Don't get burned by the same girl twice not nothing nice put that ass on ice
4 a minute represent but recognize where your true sense at.
If you don't understand shit understand this: Ain't
Know future 4 black people in this country why we are hungry
And still begging for change, change a strange word in the lives of many
Not a penny less to success and we still strewed in the game
And it a shame how black rain can leave so much rain and pain.
-Abdul Raheem

2001

I ask

By LiL

I wake up in the morning an Look
at the wall an I ask god is
this truely my down Fall, I take a
sip op her AKya release stress
a knowin That's the mess that got me in this mess

I ~~take a blunt~~ ~~taking my~~ head

I ask

Lil e

I wake up in the morning and look at the wall and ask god is this truly my downfall I take
A sip of hen tries to release stress knowing that's the mess that got me in this mess.

Never Understand me. pt 3
(the last one)

They still don't understand me, took 21 years of my life, an my grave is still empty Dear God, O. Lord tell me what is my Fate?, will I see the light, the Gate, or the Fire that Below? I have learned alot these pass couple years, lot of violece, plenty silece and a couple of tears, tryn Cope an now Jake when u. struggin on x, whats next in my tex. Y do time? is it crime?, prison time got me locked in the Chains, back 2 slavery but now body Saving me, I feel lonly in depressed, so much stress!, but I guess everything will B Fine, n due time Ill recine if I dont Loose my mind, but I'm tryin 2 b a man an stand up 2 Land, But then again if I senn, how would I win? Since my very first day on this earth I been cursed 2 Loose, But its up 2 me the route I choose, an if I prevel than Let me see hell, Dear God tell me have I fell? what is my mission on earth?, was it worth all this agony an pain? will I agan see heaven again? I'm tied an ready 2 Die, I want 2 kill my self, But why?

from the writings of Abdul Raha...
"peace be with you"

another Cry for help.

Never understand pt3

The last one

Still don't understand me took 21 yrs. of my life and my grave is still empty.

Dear god o lord tell me what is my fate? Will I see the light the gate or the fire

That belays? I have learned a lot these past couple of yrs.

A lots of violence plenty of silence and a couple of tears.

Trying to cope isn't no joke when u stressing on x what next in my text for due time.

Is it prison time got me locked in chains back to slavery

But nobodies saving me I feel lonely and depressed so much stress

But I guess everything will be fine in due time ill recline if I don't lose my mind

But I'm trying to be a man and stand up to the land.

But then again if I sin how could I win? Since my very first day on this earth

I've been cursed to loose but it's up to me the route I choose an if I fail

Than let me see hell dear god tell me have I fell?

What's my mission on earth was it worth all this drama and pain

Will I again see heaven again? I'm tired and ready to die I want to kill myself but why?

Another cry for help

2002

again   Locked up
(stop tha madness)

Da devil tricked me again. When I thought I
win I really lost. But how much did it really
cost? Not my soul I hope. I try not 2 prevoke
a bad situwation, Because of my location, where
I'm. Its kinda hard, tryA tell the guards 2
take it easy on me, Cause they B acting
kinda Fake n sleey on me. Now matter where I
go Now matter what I do, evil Lurks near through.

Temtations days R gettin nearer, I see visions
of visions, Blood poaring through a head getting
Cleaner. I try 2 compose myself an keep my
Faith in "allah" Thus if it wasn't 4 him I
would not have made it this far. I ask again
an again, Why must I Fall victom 2 a CReul
world? If I was dead there wouldn't Be know
world.

So B prepard Not Staired an
Ready 4 this Fate, Just ask yo self
this, Can U truly smile On Judgement
day.

from the aurtist of Abdula Raheem
"peace be with you"

- 34 -

Again

(stop the madness)

The devil tricked me again when I thought I won I really lost
But how much did it really cost not my soul
I hope I try not to provoke a bad situation
Because of my location where I'm kind of hard
Trying to tell these guards to take it easy on me because they act fake
And sleazy on me no matter where I go or what I do evil lurks near
through.
Temptations days are getting nearer I see vision of visions blood pouring
thru
My head getting clearer. I try to compose myself and keep my faith in
Allah
Thus if this wasn't 4 him I would have not have made it this far
I ask again and again why I must fall victim to a cruel world if I was dead
There wouldn't be known world
So be prepared not starred an ready for this fate just ask yourself this
Can u truly smile on judgment day?
Abdul Raheem

Stepmom (2 sho mma)

I thought we was cooler
than that, I was so sure,
I knew for a fact. You
was like thee mother I never
had, but the sister I always
wanted. You said I was your
son and would never be haunted.
But I guess you ~~let~~ let fear
put you in a place. I anit mad
at you just a little ~~~~ decrace.
I really looked up to you, listen
to everything you told me
I never forgot the things you
showed me so many people crossed
me plus turned they back, so
when I got bigger II payed
them back. But I never
throught you, of all people. The
love I have for you is real
I just wish it was equal, the
same from you.
                    Not fake,

                    One love,

Step mom

(2 Shonna)

I thought I was cooler than that. I was so sure I knew for a fact you were like

The mother I never had but the sister I always wanted

You said I was your son and would never be haunted

But I guess u let fear put u in place I'm not mad at cha

Just a little disgraced I really looked up to you listened to everything you told me

I never forgot the things you showed me so many people crossed me

Plus turned their backs so when I got bigger I paid them back

I never thought u of all people the love I had for you is real

I just wish it was equally the same from you not fake.

One love

Pops   (Not a poem But sorrow)

Dude was a ~~No~~ No show, I
never really new dude, He was
in the system all ~~MY~~ Life. when
he was out a met his wife.
Talk About Being trife. I tryed
to Become close to him but that
didn't work I ended up getting my
Feelings huet. as a child I was
wild & ~~Did~~ Did. Not speek muck
I hung around drug dealers Riding
Fancy cars Like Pops. ~~These~~
were people I Looked up to an wanted
to Be like, I Be like 12 years old
when I started hustling and Bustling
trya Be down. cause in my town
It was Nessasery, ~~story~~ to Some.
Pops showed me the street Life.
I Loved the ~~trill~~ trill, of Keeping
It real and Being down. But I see
Now it Wasn't worth it.

                        Maybe

Pops

(Not a poem just sorrow)

Dude was a no show I never really knew dude he was in the system all my life
When he was out I met his wife, talk about being trifling
I tried to become close to him but that didn't work
I ended up getting my feelings hurt as a child
I was feeling wild and didn't speak much I hung around drug dealers
Riding fancy cars like pops. These were people i looked up too
And wanted to be like I was like 12 years old when I started hustling and
Bustling trying to be down because in my town it's necessary
But scary to some. Pops showed me the street life
I love the trill of keeping it real and being down
But I see now it wasn't worth it
Maybe

Lying Dreams

Things still anit what they seem.
I HAVE a vistion Not a dream
and right now you Cant tell ME
nothing I dont Know, is how I'm
Feeling. Im Broke still trya stack
money to the Ceiling but I Be
Chilling Just Doing mE. I mean the
old mE I grew stronger with
timE, I took my timE still on the
grind. Im Back for everything I
own. I anit trippin, Never slippin
people Just got mE messed up, But
its Cool Cause I anit No Fool
its only when I get Caught up with
these Females I Loose. They
wont get Nothing outta mE But
2 Kids Now handle your Bisss since
you wanted it. I guess you
throught. I WAS the LamE Not
2 females Im hip too game

stop Lying

- 40 -

Lying dreams

Things still isn't what they seem I have vision not a dream and right now
you can't tell me nothing I don't know is how I'm feeling I'm broke still trying
To stack money to the ceiling but I be chilling just doing me
I mean the old me I grew stronger with time I took my time still on the grind
I'm back for everything I own I am not tripping never slipping
People just got me messed up its cool cause I am not any fool
It's only when I get caught up with these females I loose
They won't get anything out of me but 2 kids now handle your business
Since u wanted it I guess u thought I was lame. Not too females
I'm hip to the game
Stop lying

Chico Fuck all y'all
        part2   By Lih Earl

Fuck all y'all mutafuckers that fuck
with me cause on the real When the
time come 'Ima be the One Laughim
See, Laugh now, cry Later what
does that mean? really what about
(cry) tears before Laugh but who gone
cry someone? ~~All gold things~~ you
be the Fool to take that Road
but All gold dont shine and who's
world is it Not yours, damn show
Not my you sell your ~~soul~~ solle
4 a chance to Kick it and bang
But the price is much greater
than u think, nigga's dont know
me So they think that we could
Be closer than homey nigga u Foney
So stop buying drinks, and that's
Real 4 the Ol Fuck Niggas cause
they aint shit Fuck everybody and
suck a Fat dick.
        Trust in Allah

- 42 -

Fuck all yawl

Pt2

Fuck all yawl motherfuckers that fuck with me cause on the real
When the time come I'm going be the one laughing. Laugh now cry later
What about crying tears before laughter but who's gone cry?
Someone you be the fool to take that road but all gold don't shine
And whose world is it not yours damn show not
My you sell your soul for a chance to kick it and bang but
The price is much greater than u think niggas don't know me
And think we could be closer than homies, nigga you phony.
So stop buying drinks and that's real 4 the 2001 fuck niggas
Because they aren't shit and fuck everybody suck a fat dick
Trust in Allah

These Days

These Dayz Pt. 4

EveryBody talkin & Lookin' All Crazy
and Lazy as ever. ~~These Dayz~~ These Dayz
I'm tryna get mine, I'm Back on
the grind and I still ain't shine
~~Stop Fuck~~ tacking my time, I need money
in a major Way, an I ain't Fuckin
my ~~Bitch~~, cause she Broke. I
Dont smoke But Lately I Been
chieffing, mostly Stressin, Beefing
is what I Dont NEED If I dont die
~~By~~ a shot, it'll Probloly BE By a
Bag of weed. I hope it all dude
stop, they Better come get this ~~nigg~~
fo I ~~mess~~ around an hAve to Kill
this ~~nigga~~, you know what It
is and you Know who I'm talkin
Bout, these ~~niggas~~ mouth's is Running
like Fish grease. Its still a good
But Not really IN the hood is where
I Be FoR ONY ~~Motherfucka~~ Body
Looking FoR ME

These days pt. 4

Everybody is talking and looking all crazy and lazy as ever these days
I'm trying to get mine I'm back on
The grind and haven't shined. Skip talking it's my time.
I need money in a major way and I don't fuck my
Girl cause she's broke I don't smoke but have been chiefing lately
Mostly stressing beefing is what i don't
Need if I don't die by a shot it'll probably be by a bag of weed.
I hope it all stop they better come get this
Dude for I mess around and kill this dude you know what it is
And you know who I am talking about
These folks mouth is running like girls. It's still all good but not really in the hood
Is where I be if anybody
Looking for me

lying eyes

Im Not surpized cause its what they
do, and how they do it, you think you Know
a person But really they Just Refreshing,
Telling you False storys theyA play with your
mind and all the time they Lying. its Cool
Cause I never Loose my cool and still a playA
Still Straight But when These Female start
to Lie I have to shake. Thats worse
than A snich, damn and I Liked you,
tell me Why you had to BE a Lying Little
Bitch? TAlk about Being disLoyal you took
the Cake in my EYES you worse than
FAKE, Not my type, this apple is rotten
broken & Black and Im about to throw
it Back.

JACK

Lying eyes

4 MG

I'm not surprised cause it what they do and how they do it you think you
know a person
But really they just rehearsing telling you false stories trying to play with
your mind
And all the whole time lying its cool cause I never lose my cool and
I'm a playa still straight but when these females start to lie
I have to shake that's worse than a snitch damn I liked you tell me
Why you had to be a lying little bitch?
Talk about being disloyal you took the cake in my eyes you worse than fake
Not my type this applies rotten broke and black and I'm bout to throw it back.
Jack

2007

Whats New

Nothing really, people still ackin silly,
Times geting harder For some people.
my people call ME and I send them
~~For~~ pictures. ~~~~ Some ~~claim~~ to Be Broke
asking ME For ~~~~ ~~figers~~, Wondering
if Im still wht cha ~~I was~~ outcasted
U wondering how I Lasted All these
years. No more tears For mE, Just
a Little glory, a Little taste, ~~~~

I wunt the who pie, But ~~in~~ot
amelcKKKA's ~~~~ dream, more like
the E.A.R.Ls dream ~~thats~~ ~~MY~~, thing
                              my dream.

What's new?

Nothing really people still acting silly times getting harder for some people
my people
Call me and I send them pictures some claim to be broke asking for figures.
Wondering if I'm still with you I was out casted u wondering how I lasted
all these years
No more tears for me just a little glory a little taste,
I want the whole pie but not amerikkkas dream more like earls dream
That's my thing
My dream

Cheer Up.

Whats wrong sunshine? why do you
Look so gray? You Look Like you Need
some help. Let me Brighten up your
day. I know there's not 2 much 2
say I'm Not tring 2 pose, So Ima
Do it Like this heaps a Rose.

Smile. ☺

- 52 -

Cheer up

What wrong sunshine why do you look so gray you look like you need some help
Let me brighten up your day I know there's not too much to say
 I'm not trying to pose so I'm going do it like this here's a rose
Smile

Untitled

What do you want from me?
Ifs like all my life you taunt me
let me be, desinty, misery, pain
~~anger~~ anger, mama why you ack
like a stranger? I mean you
use to call, now I get know
love at all. I call you two
see how your doing plus send you
pictures, wonder if Im still
with ~~chya~~ cha, I forgive ya
But ~~I~~ I never forget. You
~~the~~ The reason I spent most of
my days geting beat.

Untitled

What do you want from me it's like all my life you taunted me let me be destiny misery pain
And anger mama why you act like a stranger?
I mean you use to call now I get no love at all I call you to see how you're doing
Plus send you pictures wondering if I'm still with you I forgive you
But I never forget you the reason I spent most of my days getting bent

Why me?

Im tied of catching cases, Im tired of white folks all in my face, Now I anit know rasit, But I have played the victim to. When I was little I never is new what to do when a white person, called me nigger. But I was never bitter I just turned my head like Martin Luther King said. I played the Back end. Thinking one day this hated agaist Blacks whould one day end. my pail skin Friend in Fouth grade, told me to Be easy. He was cool he never treating me greasy, he was real, we were kids, Just playing, he new my mama name do you know what Im saying. I wish everybody could Be like us. The world would Be very diffent

Black & White unity.

Why me?

I'm tired of catching cases I'm tired of white folks all in my face now I'm no racist
But I have played the victim too when I was little
I never knew what to do when a white person called me nigga
But I was never bitter I just turned my head like Martin Luther King Jr. said.
I played the back end
Thinking this hate against blacks would end my pail skin friend in the fourth grade
Told me to be easy he was cool he never treated me greasy
He was real we were kids just playing
He knew my mama name do you know what I'm saying
I wish everyone could be like us the world would be very different.
Black and white unity

What I am

a MAN Being Murdered same time
a Baby is Born; the Beginning and end
as far as poETRy is only Natual
that I Discrib my Name of the
essence that Defines my Name
First it was Lil Earl But times
have Change ask me Now Im the
artist for what I write might
sound plan. Took my time in the
game help my mind off Frame
Saw friends shoot up in do Lines
of cocaine. SAW my Close Friend
killed it almost torn me apart
it hurt my heart Like Huny Newton
Shot in the dark. Know more of
that please I Beg For mercy.
But who is Curse? me. Im JusT
Thirsty. For Justice I mean;
KnowLegde; its Just us. Im
tryn send my Kids to College.
When will we see the Day that
WE Can prevell? How much
moneys enough without going
to Jail.

What I am

A man being murdered same time as a baby being born,
The beginning and end as far a poetry is only natural that
I describe my name of the essence that defines my name first it was lil earl
But times have changed ask me now I'm the artist for what I write might
sound pain.
Took my time in the game kept my mind off the frame saw fiends shoot up
And do lines of cocaine saw my close friend killed and it almost tore me
apart
It hurts my heart like Huey newton shot in the dark.
Know more of that please I beg for mercy but who is cursed me?
I just trusty for justice I mean knowledge it just us
I'm trying to send my kids to college when will we see the day that we can
prevail
How money is enough without going to jail.

Leave me along

They ask me do I think I'll ever
Be At peace. No Not Really; times
is changing an' we Facing they same
prolbems. everyBody ~~~~ Still ~~~~
Staring Like marvin is what they calm,
my girl so Lame or she Just running
game. These girls is still wild ~~as~~
ever. an Its worse, they think you slow
But Im hip to everything. I dont
NEEd that drama. I got a' noff
of that From my mama. Im tryg
Live peacefully. But it seems to me
that anit gon happen No time Soon
money talks & everything else Blows
in the wind. If I die 2morrow
I'll BE Back again.

Leave me alone

They ask me do I think I will ever be at peace no not really times is changing
And we facing the same problems everybody still starving like Marvin is
what they calm
My girl so lame or she just running game these girls is still wild as ever
And its worse they think you slow but I'm hip to everything
I don't need that drama I got enough of that from my mama
I'm trying to live peacefully but it seems to me that isn't going to happen
No time soon money talks and everything else blows in the wind
If I die tomorrow I will be back again

Stop Looking at me

When I step outside and Jump
in my ride, when Im walking
with my Lady in stride, when
I Jump in the ~~_____~~ Lexus Ready
~~to flex, on my playo skills you~~
~~other Dudes pay for sex,~~

Stop looking at me

2 you haters
When I step outside and jump in my ride walking with my lady in stride.

What happen? (2 homey)
we use to Be close you was
like my Brother, Friend we
shared the same lover, New
each other since grade school
Then things started changing But I played
cool. I Never throught a woman
could come Between us, It was
all hell, you sould have seen us,
Talk About Black on black crime.
Due time came we an't seen each
other since, Last I heard
that Girl was in the club
trya get some Dead Presidents,
Damn shame. But Life goes on
and times change, its Just
messed up how a cool Person
Could turn so stange.
                    Damn.

What happened?

To my homey
We use to be close you was like my brother friend we shared the same lover
Knew each other since grade school then things started changing
But I played it cool I never thought women could come between us
It was all hell you should've seen us talking about black on black crime.
Due time came we ain't seem each other since
The last I heard that girl was in the club trying to get some dead presidents
damn shame
But life goes on and times change it just messed up
How a cool person could be so strange damn

everytime

everytime I Look At the News SomeBody gets Killed. If its Not Black on Black Crime its, war in Iraq, our troops going over there and coming Back Packed in Body Bags. Toe tags. is geting thick. Folks is shooting Folks For No reason. Im scared to let my som play out side. I Just heard about a drive-By Hit Shot too young Boys one died, overseas 25 people died From my State in one month. I meaN what are we Fighting For? what? when is it gonna emd. I hope I dont Be Next. Cause Im to young. I Just wanta RAise my sons and Be happy. to every Body out there, I think we all Need a hug.

Every time

Every time I look at the news someone is getting killed if it's not black on black crime

Its war Iraq our troops going over there and coming back packed in body bags toe tags

Getting thick folks is shooting folks for no reason I'm scared to let my son play outside

I just heard about a drive by that shot two young boys.

One died overseas today 25 die in my state in one month

I'm mean what are we fighting for what when is it going to end

I hope I don't be next because I'm too young I just want to raise my son

And be happy to everybody out there I think we all need a hug

Stop Frontin (2 Blackman)

For those of you still slangin
that ~~crack~~ poison to yo' people
Hangin around waitin. to get shot
you must of haven't Learnt Nothing
From Biggy & Pac. Two opiotions
death or Jail. ether way is hell.
You Dudes Really Need a Reality
Check, know disrespect But open
your Big ol eyes, 'an Dont Be
Surpize when that Judge Sentences
Your ~~ass~~ or you hear that Flat Line.
Cause even Nas said the World is
yours. But Who am I, I anit
~~nothin~~ Nobody 2 Listen to. Just
another Nigga ~~just~~ from the hood
Just Like you. So if you anit
gone do Nothing But sit around
Do What you do.

State of emergeny

Stop fronting

(2 Blackman)

For those of you slanging that poison to our own people hanging around
Waiting to get shot you must have not learned anything from biggie and
Pac
Two options death or jail either way is hell you dudes really need a reality
check
No disrespect but opens your big ole eyes and don't be surprised
When that judge sentences yo ass or you hear that flat line cause
Even nas said the world is yours but who am I not nobody to listen to
Just another nigga from the hood just like you doing nothing but sitting
around do what you do.

State of emergency

Reality

I try think rich, growing up
Life was a Bitch living in the
hood ant Tught me shit
So I hustle I keep my
mind and my hustle stronge
Now the cops wont leave me
along, Its like they gotta plan
For me, young Black and spiteFull
I wish allah could hold his hand
to me an Im praying that he
keep my dauthee safe I keep
two nines at the CriB and one
in my waste When Im Face with
Danger I anit know stanger

Reality

I try to think rich growing up was a bitch living in the hood did not teach
me shit
I hustle I keep my mind and muscle strong now the cops won't leave me
Alone
It's like they got a plan for me young black and spiteful I wish Allah could
Hold his hand to me and I'm praying that he keeps my daughter safe
I keep two nines at the crib and one in my waste when I'm faced with
danger
I'm no stranger

my Reaily 2010

Im Broke again got rich got Broke
again Hey I Left wisconsin Im
on my way, Still tagging along GreenBay
cant shake her and Believe me I tried
she clam she lost a Baby when my
Grandma Died oh Dear God Im tied
But anyway Im Back to the Basics
Back on my Grind I Love all
my kids thats mine, Feeling like a
want to Bust and Blow the Fuck everydes
Bout to have a mid-Life crys:
Still waiting for miss wright But Amya
to my heart so many Female want
the crown But I Love her From the
start. No Dope Sell Im Broke as
hell everyBody asking when I coming
Back, I say 2020 when cars
can Fly. Still late Night creeping
when I want too Dont check me
check yo self cause thats what
Im gon Do.

- 72 -

My reality 2010

I'm broke again got rich got broke again I left Wisconsin I'm on my way
Still tagging along green bay can't shake her believe me I tried
She claimed she lost my baby when my grandma died oh dear god
I'm tired but anyways back to basics on my grind I love all my kids that's mine
Feeling like I want to bust and blow the fuck up about to have a midlife crisis
Still waiting for the Miss Wright but Amya got my heart so many females
want the crown.
But I loved her from the start. No dope selling I'm broke as hell everybody
asking when I'm coming back I say 2020 when cars can fly
Still late night creeping when I want to don't check me check yourself cause
That's what I'm gone do.

2001

Ghetto Born Black Seed

a child that was Raised in dirt can
only whet 4 so long, But a child that
was blessed 2 vlness will soon Be free
of stress

Exit - Lil Earl
Enter - Raheem Abdul Dathumus Wright

Ghetto born black seed

A child raised in dirt can only hurt for so long and a child that was raised in mess will soon be free from stress
We still grow
Exit young e
Enter unknown

These dayz

people are still Broke, times is hard it must Be
a ReSation go get your Link card,
These dayz I'm still Laughing and crying Later
I almost Jumped in the River with a Live
alagatoir. No time For talking its about action
Now. if you anit Loving your girl Right mind
over matter gaurentee(d) gratteed SaitaFastion Now. Is
What I tell'em. These dayz Its all about the New
skip Fuck the old they Just Wanna stick Like glue,
These dayz People is Internet Cazy. But Claming
They Broke; Too Lazy. Im From the city of No
Love who needs Southern Hosiptaly I got
my own Love. Cause These Dayz Niggas will
get you and Females too, Dont ask me if Im
Broke Just do you. These dayz Im 9 to trying
it Niggaz say. I went soft But SHH!! Im
still Live in It. The Hood Still Fucked up.
my name Ring Bells Niggaz Know me Im
Bout my mail. Not Really trya Stress
wit No Female. I would Rather Bail
out Cause they Dont know me. Im older
and Colder These dayz and alot Bolder,

                                Not Lame

These days

People are still broke times is hard it must be a recession go
Get your link card these days I'm still laughing and crying later
I almost jumped in a river with a live alligator no time for talking
It's about action now if you aren't loving your girl right mind over matter
Guaranteed satisfaction now is what I tell 'em these days it's all about new shit
Fuck the old they just want to stick to you like glue. These days' people are
internet crazy
But claiming there broke too lazy. I'm from the city of no love fuck Southern
Hospitality because these days' niggas will get you and females too.
Don't ask me if I'm broke just do you. These days I'm nine to fiving it niggas
Think I went soft but I'm still live in it. The hoods still fucked up my name
ring bells
Niggas know me I'm about my mail. Not really trying to stress with no female
I would rather bail out because they don't know me. I'm older and colder
These days and a lot bolder
Not lame

I got a Story to tell

Started off Love making turning to hot sex ⬤ They sexing For two hours straight to He realize He was Late. OK Hes gone Now. Six hours past Hes home Now. She kisses Him When He walks thru the door But Hes a Little tied No more. She starts Raming on an on about Him Being gone so much, she says He Fucking around and throws the First Punch. Boom!! Chairs Flying Vases, tables, He's telling her Calm down Be stable, Shes cursing and screaming too the neighbors here. Po'po's Kick IN the door all clear, Shes sobbing and crying From ear to ear. He goes to County problems disappear, She calms she is so down is all Hes thinking Damn and the Fucked up part They Wasnt even DrinKin. Teying to make Bail But cant He For got he Left his money in the Bank, meanwhile she on Some other shit Fuck sticking around she packed the kids up and hit town. Now shes Chasing New dick Back to her old self meanwhile he's thinking I hope the po'po's Didnt Find that gun on the Shelf. So the moral of the story is this if you break up with a Bitch do it from good lenth.

4 Real.

I got a story to tell

Started off love making turning to hot sex they sexing for two hours straight
Till he realizes he was late. Ok he gone now six hours past he is now home
She kisses when he walks thru the door but he's a little tired no more
She starts rambling on about him being gone so much
She says he fucking around and throws the first punch boom!!
Chairs flying Vases and tables he's telling her to calm down
Be stable she cursing and screaming that the Neighbors hear
Popo's kicking in the door all clear she sobbing and crying from ear to ear
He goes to county problems disappear she calms she is so down is
All he thinking damn and the fucked up part they wasn't even drinking trying to make
Bail but can't he forgot he left his money in the bank meanwhile
She on some other shit fuck sticking around she packed the kids up and
Hit town now she chasing new dick back to her old self meanwhile
He's thinking I hope the po pos didn't find that gun on the shelf so the moral of the story is this if you break up with your bitch do it from A GOOD LENGTH.
- 4 REAL.   (true story)

Kimora

So young and Joycefull Full of life, It hurts me
to write this My heart took A Knife. I Never
Really Knew You But I still Fill your pain maybe because
its Black call me insane, I dont care the very throught
of you Lying there why People stalke makes me shed
a tear I mean tears through out the history of
all my 30 years have I ever Knew I Baby so young
to perish. Its true Niggaz die everyDay But Not
Like this Imia say it Foour More times You will
Be Missed; and they Never knew u Couldnt even
telAvise what a Damn shame But Not a
Surpise. and we got a Black President Now!
I guess he Never Knew either. Some Leader of
the Free World. But Back to the story how
old was the Lil girl? Two!! GodDamN!!
But I Bet they make a Big Deal about
Linzey Loham or Jay z Next CD. But I
will Never Forget you Kimora Not me. please
take care of Your BaBys teach are Kids
especially Black Live Your life to
the Fullest cause will you Die ant
Know coming Back.

                    unless you 2pac

Kimora

So young and Joyce full of life it hurts me to write this my heart took a knife
 I never really knew you but i still feel your pain maybe because its black call
me insane
I don't care the very thought of you lying there why people stair makes me
shed a tear
I mean tears throughout history of all my thirty years have I ever knew I baby
so young to perish Its true niggas die every day but not like this I'm going
to say it four more times
You will be missed and they never knew u couldn't even televise.
What a damn shame but not a surprise and we got a black president
Now I guess he never knew either, some leader of the free world but back to
the story
How old was the little girl? TWO!!!! GOD DAMN!!!!
But I bet they make a big deal about Lindsey low ham or Jay Z next cd But I
will never forget you kimora not me. Please take care of your babies Teach are
kids especially black live your life to the fullest Cause when you die there's
no coming back.
Unless you Tupac.

make a wish

1 I wish I had a Better Job
2 I wish Sometimes my Girl wasn't such a Sob'
3 I wish I had Bill Gates money
4 I wish in ten YEars I Be Laughing Like this shit Funny
5 I wish I Didnt hade to twork,
6 I wish Females wouldn't complain about getting they Feelings hurt.
7 I wish my Kids Could one Day 'see what I see Living Life struggling in this White man World.
8 I wish my Kids Never struggle, I rather see them grow up to throw up, all mustle.
9 I wish my Father Never WENt to Jail when I was three cause that Right there is was make me too a G.
10 I wish I would have Loved her Like She wanted.
11 I wish that the pages in this Book wont Be haunted,
12 I wish I would have seen my Garandma Face to Face Before she DiE I will Never Forget that Nite I cryed
13 I wish they could remember,
14 I wish every month was SeptemBer.
15 I wish I didnt have to write this, whats Next I writting my hit List.
16 I wish It was peace I mean real peace in chicago, my hood Your hood wehre: ever I go
17 I wish the World Blow up tell obama Push the Button, and we come Back fow 8

- 82 -

Make a wish

1. I WISH I HAD A BETTER JOB.

2. I WISH MY GIRL SOMETIMES WASN'T SUCH A SOB.

3. I WISH I HAD BILL GATES MONEY.

4. I WISH IN TEN YEARS I BE LAUGHING LIKE THIS SHIT FUNNY.

5. I WISH I DIDN'T HAVE TO WORK.

6. I WISH FEMALES WOULDN'T COMPLAIN ABOUT GETTING THERE FEELINGS HURT.

7. I WISH MY KIDS COULD ONE DAY SEE WHAT I SEE LIVING LIFE STRUGGLING IN THIS WHITEMANS WORLD.

8. I WISH MY KIDS NEVER STRUGGLE I RATHER SEE THEM GROW UP TO THROW UP, ALL MUSTLE.

9. I WISH MY FATHER NEVER WENT TO JAIL WHEN I WAS THREE CAUSES THAT RIGHT THERE IS WHAT MADE ME TO G.

10. I WISH I WOULD HAVE LOVED HER LIKE SHE WANTED.

11. I WISH THAT THESE PAGES IN THIS BOOK WONT BE HAUNTED

12. I WISH I WOULD HAVE SEEN MY GRANDMA FACE TO FACE BEFORE SHE DIED I WILL NEVER FORGET THE NITE I CRIED

13. I WISH THEY COULD REMEMBER

14. I WISH EVERY MONTH WAS SEPTEMBER

15. I WISH I DIDN'T HAVE TO WRITE THIS WHATS NEXT I WRITE MY HIT LIST.

16. I WISH IT WAS PEACE I MEAN REAL PEACE IN CHICAGO IN MY HOOD YOUR HOOD WHERE EVER I GO

17. I WISH THE WORLD BLOW UP TELL OBAMA TO PUSH THE BUTTON AND WE COME BACK TORE UP

MAKE A WISH II

1 I wish my mama Live Longer than ~~me~~ call me
Selifish But I dont wanta she my mama getting
curried.

2 I wish I Never had to sell crack

3 I wish there Never was crack

4 I wish when you Look at me you Dont
Just see Black.

5 I wish Kimora Didnt have to Die she was
to young, Please somebody tell me why?

6 I Wish people wouldnt hate.

7 I wish people ~~were~~ not so Fake.

8 I wish everybody was gay, then the world
would Be happy, Not nappy. we straight

9 I wish it was only one race, one color
For every one wit a Diffent Face.

10 I wish when they think of the Good Book they
think of the "Quran" Holy Cause Power is money
and time Just moves on.

11 I wish ME and my enemys could trade shoes
For one week,

12 I wish me and her could speak on some Real
ness. I still Kiss is all we do For Real miss.

13 I wish Shorty Stop ~~stairing~~ at me cause
she dont its Prolbey gone turn to a mis
understand.

- 86 -

MAKE A WISH 2

1. I WISH MY MAMA LIVE LONGER THAN ME CALL ME SELFISH BUT I DON'T WANT TO SHE MY MAMA GETTING CURRIED

2. I WISH I NEVER HAD TO SELL CRACK

3. I WISH THERE NEVER WAS CRACK

4. I WISH WHEN YOU LOOK AT ME YOU JUST DON'T SEE BLACK

5. I WISH KIMORA DIDN'T HAVE TO DIE SHE WAS TOO YOUNG PLEASE SOMEBODY TELL ME WHY?

6. I WISH PEOPLE DIDN'T HATE

7. I WISH PEOPLE WERE NOT SO FAKE

8. I WISH EVERYBODY WAS GAY THEN THE WORLD WOULD BE HAPPY, NOT NAPPY WE STRAIGHT

9. I WISH IT WAS ONLY ONE RACE ONE COLOR FOR EVERYONE WIT DIFFERENT FACES

10. I WISH WHEN THEY THINK OF THE GOOD BOOK THE THINK OF <u>THE HOLY QURAN</u> CAUSE POWER IS MONEY AND TIME JUST MOVE ON

11. I WISH ME AND MY ENEMIES COULD TRADE SHOES FOR A ONE WEEK

12. I WISH ME AND HER COULD SPEAK ON SOME REALNESS A STILL KISS IS ALL WE DO FOR REAL MISS

13. I WISH SHORTY STOP STARRING AT ME CAUSE IF SHE DON'T IT'S PROBABLY GONNA TURN INTO A MISS. UNDERSTAND.

ENLOGUE exit.

2007

We on the Block chilling, Fiends smoking rocks fling; Some dude Just got shot. his Grams Called the Cops. So the Block Cleared out. Now I'm Back At the house, Back in the Crib For those of you wanna Know how a playa Live. Lil kids Runing around tearing stuff up. my girl Chilling waiting to get plucked. we dont worry about outsiders, we they are mostly quiet. Tey not to start riots. moms is acting Distart Know phone calls Know visit. pops on another game. I Dont Know if he runing game or he think somebody lame. Family Members come in go. They with you First till you Broke. you Know, or so they think. Know more BaBy mamma drama. I'm done with that a chapter, I Live For my Sons From Now to the years to come. I PRAY My dauther is safe. in dew time everything will FALL in its place.

OVER ⮑

People still asking me For thangs. But get mad when I let them hang. I dont worry about it. Cause Ima get mines; might take a little time. But Im trying. you dudes step to me Just know your place dont get outta Line. I dont worry about where I currently reston. and If I got money. Cause the world is still mine.

Epilogue

We on the block chilling fiends smoking rocks pilling, some dude just got shot

Ms. Grams called the cops.so the block cleared out now I'm back at the house

Back at the crib for those who want to know how a playa live

Kids running around tearing stuff up.my girl chilling waiting to get plucked

We don't worry about outsiders we keep our mouths quite try not to start a riot

Moms is acting distant, know phone calls know visits.

Pops on another game I don't know if he running game or he thinks someone's lame.

Family members come and go, they with you first till you broke.

You know. Or so they think no more baby mama drama I'm done with that chapter

I live for my sons from now to the years to come i pray my daughter is safe

In due time everything will fall in place. People are asking me for things

But get mad when I let them hang. I don't worry about it because I'm going to get mines

Might take a little time but I'm trying. You dudes step to me just know your place

Don't get out of line don't worry about where I currently resign and if I got money

Cause the world is mine.

Love Is Black

Love you, (2 grandma Wright)
u took me from my mama
when I was little bring on along. cause
you knew that my mama was know
where near grown. Mama was young
Really young some may say she was
sprung. You Raised me like I came
From you, well I guess I did, your
kids where damn Near grown so Its
Safe to say I was your only
kid. We were close. I use to love
when you cook for me. You
Introduced me to Church. I
was so passionit about it. Because
I was involved in something. you
taught me something. you was and
will always be my Faviote grandma
I still watch the news Like you
told me, and I Never For got
everything you showed me. And
For that I Just Wanta say
thank you,

Love you

(2 grandma wright)

U took me from my mama when I was a little baby an along because

You knew my mama was nowhere near grown mama was young really young

Some may say sprung you raised me like I came from you well I guess I did

Your kids were grown so it's safe to say I was your only kid we were close

I used to love when u cooked for me you introduced me to church

I was so passionate about it because I was involved in something you taught me

Something you will always be my favorite grandma

I still watch the news like you told me and

I will never forget everything you showed me

And for that I thank you

miss you 2 grandma miller Praqline

I Never really New you at First
but when I Finally met you It
was like heaven. I was so happy.
me Lookin all nappy, out of All your
grandKids you New I was speical
I hate that you gone but I Know
gods gonna Bless you. Your son
Said NoBody cryed at You're Funaral
Well thats a lie ; Because I cryed so
hard inside I could of hade a heart
attack. I miss you MRs miller I
want you Back. I wish you could
See your greatgRandKids , I Know
You watching over me, Keeping
mE safe So when my day Finally
ComE WE could exchange place.

Love you

"God Bless the dead"

Miss you

2 grandma Pearline Miller

I never really knew you at first but when I finally met you it was like heaven

I was so happy me looking all nappy out of all your grandkids you knew

I was special I hate that you are gone but I know god has blessed you your son said

No one cried at the funeral but that's a lie I cried so hard inside

I could have had a heart attack I miss you Mrs. Miller I want you back

I wish you could see your great grandkids I know you're watching over me

Keeping me safe so that when my day come we could exchange place

Love you

Flowers in your hair.

So Beautiful, You Look So Right
I Loved you when my eye
First Caught sight. You Like a
Don's wife prefect in every way.
Sometimes I dont know what
you see in me Becides my
dou my hay. I Never trick, ok
maybe a Little Bit. But you
worth every pennie mean every
dollar. You Never ask me For
Nothing thats why I Love you
alot of people in my Life But a
~~xxxx~~ No one above you. Like ~~~~
Black dove, I keep you iN my
mind, Like ever Lasting Love
I hope this Last For a
Life time. So Dont cry or
Beware I hope you Like the
Flowers that I ~~got you~~
For your hair.

Flowers in your hair

So beautiful you look so right I loved you when my eye first caught sight

You like a don's wife perfect in every way sometimes

I don't know what you see in me besides my doe I never trick okay

Maybe a little bit but you're worth every penny I mean every dollar

You never ask me for nothing that's why I love you a lot of people in my life

But no one above you like a black dove I keep you in my mind like everlasting love

I hope this last a life time so don't cry or beware

I hope you like the flower I got for your hair.

ee

Girlfriend (2 shay)

But **Not** Like you think We was
Just cool tight Like a Blink.
We kicked it everyday we knew
each other we was close, you
Was like my Brother, Nothing
other than a cuz Relationship ~~went~~ ~~smoked~~
on trips all off us, we ~~smoked~~
sometimes I Never tell yo mama
You cuss. You was like the Lil
Sister I Never had, But the
Girlfriend I always wanted, But
I guess will Never Know cause
my past is Forever Haunted.

One Love
stay Real. Trill
Family

- 98 -

Girlfriend

2 shay

But not like you think we just cool tight like a blink we kicked it every day

We knew each other we were close you was like my brother

Nothing other than a cousin relationship went on trips all of us

We smoked sometimes never tell your mama you cussed

You was like a little sister I never had but the girlfriend I always wanted

But I guess we will never know because my love forever is haunted.

White girls
2001
Love or Lust? part.1
by. mr Cool

She partys all the time stays
out all night Loves two kick it
and smoke weed all on a
saturday night I try to look pass it
and just be a playa, Thinkin of the
days when I was thinkin, ain't much playa
Whats up with these hoes wanta cool
nigga but cant handle the cool
nigga better stick with the lames
if u trya get paid, Lookin 4
Love but u ain't got it made.
Think Ima sweet for writing this
Far From Baby just givin game
and hoping maybe u ~~guess~~ take
notes or somein, I ~~guess~~ its
true what they say. (Ha-Ha) but
all the time Im wondering if
my baby okay. Peace
mr. Cool is back

White girls

Love or lust?

She parties all the time stays out all night loves to kick it and smoke weed

All on a Saturday night I try to look past it and just be a playa thinking of the days

When I was thuging isn't much playa what's up with these hoes want a cool nigga

But can't handle the cool figure better stick with them lames if you trying to get paid

Looking for love but you don't got it made think I'm sweet for writing this far from it baby

Just giving game and hoping you take notes or something I guess it's true what they say

Ha-ha but at the same time wondering is my baby okay

Mr. Cool is back

4 Phat
Phat

I use to Love you g g y

● U use to Be tru, we use
to Be tight Like glue. ● WE use
to hold hands ~~in~~ the park, Late
night Kissing ~~after~~ dark. You
say I stole yo heart, I say you
Just got Lost in the dark. its
a shame how we fell apart
We started off secret Lovers
~~Under~~ under cover than you Be
came my girl. I took you
to my hood LEt you See how
a playa Live you understood
What ~~my~~ life style is. Then
things got ~~cover~~ Shady you tryed
to have my BaBy, tryed to
play ME. Couldn't let you fade me
so I had ~~to~~ Shake you.

- 102 -

I used to love you

(2 CY aka phat phat)

You used to be tight like glue we use to hold hands in the park

Late night kissing after dark

You say I stole your heart I say you just got lost in the dark

It's a shame how we fell apart we started off secret lovers under the covers

Then you became my girl I took you to my hood let you see how a playa live

you understood how my lifestyle is Then things got shady you tried to play me
by having my baby couldn't let you play me So I had to shake you
Love lost

? LOVE Pt.4

Everybody wants to come up, But
Dont Know body Want too Be down
Females 2Day is so cazy so Lazy
What a nigga gotta Do to find
someone true that will say with
a nigga thru thick & thin, you
really dont Love me and I see it
So clear, Im done with Them I
Had fun with them, my son with dem
Ima pop a Bottle and see them 2morrow
my Love was only Borrowed I am
not a Fool, I Just took Hoes to
school, play By the Rules But know
Body Does thats why I dont
play games, thats for Lames

Love pt. 3

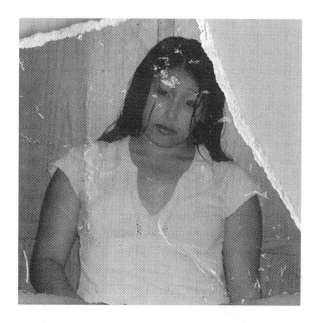

Everybody wants to come up but don't know body want to be down

Females today is so crazy and lazy what a man got to do to find someone true

That will stay with a brother thru thick and thin? You really don't love me

And I see so clear I'm done with them I had fun with them my son with them

I'm a pop a bottle and see them tomorrow maybe my love was only borrowed

I am not a fool I just took little girls to school play by the rules but nobody does

That's why I don't play games thats for lames

O the Joy of Life
Black & Brown
Nice, sweet, palm trees
No City Lights, No interuptions
too Nite. Its Just me and you
ME and my Baby. How can I Be.
Whole? Without You, there
is No me; is how it supose
to Be. You my girl, your suBpose
to Be close to me By my side
Before Next to kin and Like
mexicans We Back at it
again. So we sex again and
again and again, and then every thang is
Cool, WAKE up in the morning
and take the kids to school.
No Prolbems, No Worries,
in No hurry to Leave each
other, you my wife my first
and only real miss Wright.
Im Just saying who ever has
that Life. I wonder, Must
Be Nice.

Fansl

- 106 -

O the joy of life

Nice, sweet, palm trees no city lights no interruptions to night

It's just me and you   my baby how can I be whole

Without you there is no me is how it's supposed to be you my girl

You supposed to be close by my side before next of kin and like Mexicans

We back at it again. So we sex again, again and again and then

Everything cool wake up in the morning and take the kids to school

No problems no worries in no hurry to leave each other's side

Your my wifey first and only real Miss Wright

I'm just saying who ever has that life must be nice

Fantasy

girl of my dreams

Where have you Been? I've Been Dreaming
again. Thinking of you, Wondering what
would I Do with out you. Hoping
when I meet you, you are just Like
my dreams. Beatiful & as Black as
me. I picture you with hip's & thighs
that Could shake the night, with
a Booty that is so Big It could Blind
the sight. Now thats a real ms. Right.
So girl of my dreams where ever you
are I hope you are close An not
2 Far.
            woman.

based on a Real dream

Girl of my dreams

Where have you been I've been dreaming again thinking of you wondering?

What I would do without you hoping when I meet you are just like my dreams

Beautiful and as black as me I picture you with hips and thighs that shake the night

With booty so big I could blind the sight now that's a real Miss Wright

So girl of my dreams where ever you are I hope you are close and not too far

Women

(Based on a real dream)

My unForgotten Chidd
(Amya Wright)
I Loved you Before You
Was Born. I Knew You
Would Look Like me. I wish
I was around you so you could
see what type of person I
am. I Never ment to hurt you.
You where so young. I Never
Really Knew you yet in still I
was sprung. Not I day goes
By that I Dont think about
you. Nobody in this World could
tell me I dont. I wish we
Could Be together Right Now
But we prolbuly Wont. I hope
you Dont Forget me cause I
will Never Forget you. You
is my one truely Ms. Wright
I Just Wish you Knew.

I Never Forget you! For real

My unforgotten child

4 Amya S. Wright

I loved you before you born I knew you would look like me

I wish you was around me to see what type of a person I am

I never meant to hurt you. You were so young I never really knew you

Yet in still I was sprung not a day goes by that I don't think of you

Nobody in this world could tell me I don't I wish we could be together rite now

But we probably won't I hope you don't forget me cause I will never forget you,

You is my one truly first Ms. Wright I just wish you knew

For real

I never forget you

To my unborn child

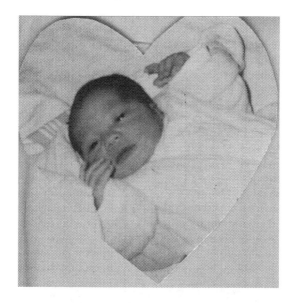

What more can I say since the very first day I fell in love with you

But I got to tell you watch what you mama does its drama do you

You just haven't reached that age and when you die if you famous they put you on the front page

I had a homey die last year from a 12 gage it's like we living in a cage

I isn't talking about jail shit that's hell don't ever go there then they really got you

Don't get to caught up with material things just be cool cause what inside you is

 Inside me.

2 my UnBorn Child
part 2

What more can I say. Since the
Very first day. I fell in Love
with you. But I gotta tell you,
WAtch what your MAMA do. Its
dRAMA do, you Just Anit Reach that
Age, and when you die, if
you Famous, they put you on
The FRont Page. I had a homey
died Last week From a 12 gage
Its Like we Living in a Cage, and
I anit talking Bout Jail ; shit thats Hell.
dont ever go there, then they
Really got you. dont get 2
a-tacks 2 these Lil Chichen
Heads, cause they all Dead, Just
Be Cool and Be you. Cause whats
in you -/s inside me.

To my unborn child

pt. 2

What more can I say since the very first day I fell in love with you

But I got to tell you watch what you mama does its drama do you

You just haven't reached that age and when you die if you famous they put you on the front page

I had a homey die last year from a 12 gage it like we living in a cage

I isn't talking about jail shit that's hell don't ever go there then they really got you

Don't get to attached to these chicken heads because they all dead just be cool and be you

Cause what's inside you is inside me

ghetto poet:

👁 c u

Still sexy.

I see you still got it. I Dont Dout it.
With your $1000 dollar weeve, Big Booty,
BaBy Daddy Name tatted on your Sleeve
Looking Like you anit Been ~~Fucked~~ topched
IN a while, ~~fuck~~ mess with me I Bet
I give that ass ~~a~~ smile. You Know
how I Do. I Wont Sin one on mess with
me ma; Lets drink some gin OR
maybe some HeN, But then again ~~I~~ Skip
the Liqour I Just Look at that
ass once & watch my ~~pants~~ get
bigger. I know you got a man
an thats cool, I got a woman
But Dont Be know Fool. Thats old
News & this is Now. Yo' man ~~Fuckin~~ doing
you Right?, I Dont see how. Why you
So BoRed? I Bet You anit Ready
Fok what I gott IN stoRed. IF
you think I'm Playing games you
Betta stick with the Lames, cause
I got ~~this~~! the city is mine Relax
yo' mine.

Still shining

Just Look at my diamonds

Still sexy

I see you still got it I don't doubt it with your 1000 dollar weave big booty

Baby daddy name tatted on your sleeve looking like you haven't been touched
in a while

I bet I give that ass a smile you know how I do I won't sin come on chill with
me

Ma lets drink some gin or maybe some hen but then again skip the liquor

I just took a look at the ass and my pants got bigger I know you got a man
and that's cool

I got a women but don't be know fool that's old news and this is now you're
man doing you rite

I don't see how why you so bored I bet you isn't ready for this and what i
got in stored

If you think I'm playing games you better stick with the lames cause
I got this the city is mine so relax your mind
Still shinning
Just look at my diamonds

'84

Too Hip Hop
tRue Luv.

When I FiRst Fell in Love wit You It
Had 2 be "94 when I FiRst heard 2pac & Biggie
Flow, I mean I can think Back in the
dayz IN "84 when LL cool J and Run D.M.C
use to go, man they WAS Rippin it Up, tAlkin
bout being wild we Use 2 get Buck, since
'94 I Realized what my culture Is, that
hip hop is me and the FuRtuRe of my kids,
this Long NeveR Ending Fight agaist poverty
aint Nothing changed people Just Robing me!,
When are we gonna leaRn? We keep getting BuRned
by the same Ho's twice Knockin us down an what
we SacaFice? CuRe Souls stay cold as Ice,
Living LiFe trys do Right! help us, Luv us,

To hip hop "84

When I first fell in love with you it had to be in 94 when I first heard 2pac and Biggie

Flow I mean I can think back in the day in 84 when LL Cool J and run DMC

Used to go man they was ripping it talk about being wild we used to get buck

Since then I realized what my culture is that hip hop is me and future of my kids

This is a long never ending fight against poverty ain't nothing changed people still robbing

When are we going to learn we keep getting burned by the same girl?

Knocking us down and what are we sacrificing are souls stay cold as ice living life

Trying to do right help us love us

PRETTY BROWN BROWN

4 Erica

Too All my Honeys that Roll
Blunts up -But dont Smoke,
the ones that see some in you When
you Broke, the ones thats down.
There thru thick n thin. Closer
than kin realer than a Friend.
I know What that feels like, it feels
right, cant have No girl all up on me,
Its hard to mess Wit somebody after
she touches me. I Love to see
her in a Black skirt, she makes
me smile when she tryes to Flirt.
But I dont say much, Im Just happy
Wit her touch

Keep Lovin me

Pretty Brown

2 ERICA

To all my honeys that roll blunts up and don't smoke the ones who see something in you

When you broke the ones that down thru thick and thin closer than kin realer

Than a friend I know what that feels like it feels right can't have a girl all up on me

It's hard to mess with someone after she touches me I love to see her in that black skirt

She makes me smile when she tries to flirt I don't say much
I'm just happy with her touch
Keep loving me baby

White Love

2 stephanee

Sorey too Be the one to
tell you this But we thru, over
done, I wish I had a son, But
thats daddys girl, who u wit
then made me drop a seed
yall need too quit, you 3 your
mama, all yall is, is drama
and am tried of that, shit
I might as well Be fuckin' wit
a hoodrat, she say she tells little
white lies, I can see it in her eyes
Such a ~~____~~ ugly Face, I wish I
Could, I need somin thick Big, and Juicy,
Fatt ass nice and Brown, where
we at BaBy", she ask me, The
"The Hamthons" I say, Come here BaBy Lets
sit down and ~~____~~ prey oh

yours trully,

[signature]

the pearl

White love

4 Stephanie

Sorry to be the one to tell you this but we thru over done

I wish I had a son but that's daddy little girl who you got

I slipped and dropped a seed yawl need to quit

You and your mama all yawl is drama and I'm tired of that

Shit I might as well be messing with a hood rat
She says she still tells little white lies I can see it in her eyes
Such an ugly face I wish I would again
I need something thick big juicy
P.h.a.t ass nice brown and round
You know

ME & her

2 munLetu

wasnt really soppose to Be
WE started off cool & Friendly.
I Did Not picture it would go
this Far, But Im glad it did and
Love are Kids. oppistes do atact.
How real is that, So much B.S
Between me & her, people Didnt Wanta
see us together, but thru the
Weather we proved thick & thin.
I Never Knew a Love So true; maybe
once. I am a man wit a plan
and NEED a Woman to Be my
QUEEN, without her I can not Be
King.

Signed. King

Me & her

2 M

Wasn't really supposed to be we started off cool &friendly

I didn't picture it would go so far but I'm glad it did

And I love are kids opposites do attract

How real is that? So much bull shit between me and her

People didn't want to see us together

But thru the weather we proved thick and thin

I never knew a love so true

May be once

I am a man with a plan

And need a woman to be my queen

Without her I cannot be king

Tha Perfect (Break up)

What more can you ask for
I'm straight. more than that,
Never Late when I wanna Be
Because of me you know what
real Love is. Real Kings handle
they Biss, Remember this, in that
Rental Car, you was wild as hell
At First it was a one nite
thang turned eight months. We
Smoked stail Blunts and Bullshited
them I shited On you, you got
pregnant, I chilled with my Baby
you walking round town Lookin Crazy
Then I went away and got Knoked
you Did more shit For me than
most Muthafucka's Did in a Lifetime
when I was in Jail so I got
out n Married you carryed you For
a Few months We Fought
So much that things Fell apart.
I Loved you so much that you
could Not take it But i$s
Cool cause I know Next time my
time Dont waste it.

                    See y.

The perfect

(break up)

What more can you ask for I'm straight more than that never late

When I want to be because of me you know what real love is

Real kings handle there business remember this when in that rental car

You were wild as hell at first it was a one night thing turned into eight months!
We smoked stale blunts and bull shitted then I shitted on you. You got pregnant
I chilled with my baby you were walking around town looking crazy.
Then I got knocked you did more for me than most muthafuckas did in my
whole lifetime
When I was in jail. I got out married you, carried you for a few months we fought
so much that we fell apart. I loved you so hard you couldn't take it, but its cool
cause next time
I know don't waste it See you

Love is Still Black

Waking up next to you thats a plus Love
I hope you still got my Back Love that a
Must having 3 or 4 of my kids is not enough
Love I Need your heart & soul too Untouched
Love . Instead of giving me a case Love taking
that damn thang Rather see me Balling than
to Let your Love hang, Still aint got know Friends
But you still Riding we move away In a Small
town and go into hiding Rather you Black or
Brown It Dont matter Love serve me that
Ice on a warm platter I saw her with her
BabyFather But It Dont matter Since she
gave me the pussy that ass is getting phatter
But I aint gon sress Love I Rather Sex
Love and Bless Love I Love when we
In the Sheets you the Best Love

Keep Loving me

Thick or thin

Love is still black

Waking up next to you love that's a plus love I hope you still got my back love that's a must.

Having 3 or 4 of my kids is not enough love I need your heart and soul too untouched

Love instead of giving me a case love taking that damn thang rather see me balling

Than to let your love hang Shit don't got no friends but you still riding

We move away in a small town and go into hiding

Rather you black or brown it don't matter love serve me that ice on a warm platter

I saw her with her baby's father but it doesn't matter since she gave me that pussy

That ass is getting phata but I'm not going to stress love I'd rather sex love

Bless love I love when we in the sheets you the best love

Keep Love me

Thick or thin
Follow up to love is black {da sequel}

uncondiontal LOVE (Rahiesha)

WHEN you was First BORN I did Not even Like you
But I grew to Love u, I Remember what my Father
told me, Its uncondiontal Love, between us. Its So
amazing How I watched you grow From a BaBy
to a Now young Lady. You super smart and
Beautiful you. will always have my heart My
First sister my twin From the start. I will always
have yo Back Know matter what. I Hope you Live
your Life, Live it up. To the Fillest. Dont stress
over Know pety mess Just do you, on time things
will come. Trust me. if you want real hard
watch your dreams come true. Dreaming of
riches is something I dont Do. I Dream For
my Kids which is you, I dream For my grandkids
30 years From Now I dream and hope I will stay
Be around, I Know you will Be sussvsfull at what
even you Do. Cause its in your Blood to stay true. We
grew up A Thug Life Living ruff and Raw Not to
mention the things we saw. I Was blinded as a
youth Know one Really told me the truth and they
tried to take my Figga's so I kelp my weight up with
my hate an paid them Back when I got Bigger.
Now I Laugh at a Nigga that ask me For
Shit. I Laugh So hard they run quick, I made a
New Family Now and Im Fucus my time is money
So my words is soft Spoken. My New Family
is New Now its ██████ 2000 something so u
Know its Brand New Now

Still Loving that Black   Baby sis
WOMEN

Unconditional love

(4 Rahiesha)

When you were first born I did not even like you but I grew to love you
I remember what my father told me its unconditional love between us
It's so amazing how I watched you grow from a baby to now a young lady
you super smart
And beautiful you will always have my heart my first sister my twin from
the start
I will always have your back know matter what. I hope you live your life,
Live it up to the fullest don't stress over no petty mess just do you in time
things will come
Trust me if you want real hard watch your dreams come true
Dreaming of riches is something I don't do I dream for my kids which is
you
I dream for my grandkids 30 years from now I dream and hope I will still
be around
I know you will be successful at whatever you do because it's in your blood
to stay true
We grew up a thug life living ruff and raw not to mention the things we
saw
I was blinded as a youth no one really told me the truth and they tried to
take my figgas'
So I kept my weight up with my hate and paid them back when I got bigger
now
I laugh at a nigga when they ask me for shit I laugh so hard they run away
Quick I made a new family now and I'm focused
My time is money so my word is soft spoken my new family is knew now
its
2000 something so you know it's brand new now
Baby sis
Still loving that black women

Soul &Heart

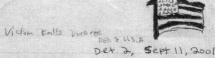

Victim falls here
Det 2 U.S.A
Det 2, Sept 11, 2001

I Look in the mirrow, I stand tall,
5 Feet 4 put my back aqost the wall,
I often Ponder 3 wonder about Life,
Innocent victims fall victim 2 police profoundly,

But the reilaty is Blacks killin Blacks,
We search 4 world peace an have not Fount it
in it own back yard, an everyday we wonder why
Life is so, hard,

Liberty

As for 2 the sky an ask god why, Do it have 2 b this way,
Black people & White people need 2 come 2gEther & pray,
4 a better day, New light, Something tight, down 2 the sole,
It was told, not 2 Fold down 2 evil, And I know try
Not 2 Lie we will do alright,

So America let us Fight the good fight & stay tight
in peace, and decrease the vengence, & tendere amone each other,
word 2 mutha, gotta LUV her, 21 years and Im still
sleepin under the cover,

Stay tru 2 each other, thats re strench, keep it movin
Like the Jews, 2 a high Length, Peace be out from
above, this Raheem witt much LUV.

from the writings Abdul Raheem
peace be witt you

2002

Victim falls nearer (dedicated 2 U.S.A)

September 11, 2001

I look in the mirror I stand tall
5 feet 4 inches tall with my back against the wall
I often ponder & wonder about life
Innocent victims fall prey to police brutality
But the reality is blacks killing blacks
We search 4 world peace and have not for it in our own back yards
And every day we wonder why life so hard?
We look 2 the sky an ask god why do it have to be this way
Black people & white people need 2 come together & pray
4 a better day new light something tight down 2 the soul it was told not to
fold down 2 evil
And if we try not to lie we will do alright
 So America let us fight the good fight & stay tight
In peace and decrease the vengeance & tendency among each other word 2
mother got to luv her 21 years and I'm sleeping under the cover
Stay keeping it moving like the Jews 2 a high length peace is out from above
this Raheem wit much luv.
From the writings Abdul Raheem
"Peace be with you"

Katrina *ded 2 New Orleans* (2006)
Before we Self Destruct

Why you do US Like that BaBy?
I mean us (Blacks) out of all people.
We Suppose to Be equal. First
9/11 and now this. damn!! Is are
Skin Color are Bliz? if it is
~~~~ then we as sure dead than 400
years ago. Whats next For us?
WE Need a ReVolution, I mean a
Real reVolution. People talk But dont
Do Nothing. They just sit around
Frontin. Anther Black person gets
Killed and makes the Second Page
Sonner or later we wont Be
able to hold all the Rage.

                                   I hope

    "Before we self Destruct"

Katrina

Dedicated to New Orleans (2006)

Before we self-destruct why do us like this baby?

Why do us like that baby?

I mean us (blacks) out of all people.

We supposed to be equal

First 9/11 and now this. Damn!! Is Skin color are bliss?

If it is than we are as sure dead as 400 years ago

We need a revolution

I mean a real revolution. People talk but don't do anything. They just sit around fronting

Another black person gets killed and makes the second page

Sooner or later we won't be able to hold the rage.

I hope "Before we self-destruct"

2007

-Goverment-   Bush
                    2 mr ~~Benefit~~

please stop lying Saying what
you gonna Do? Because I see
things From a diffect VEIW.
my nieborhood still messed up
We still dying From drugs over
run By thugs, White Folks showing
No Love. and it gets worse
its Like Being Black is a Curse
in AmeickKKia, I ant scared of
Ya, you killed my hero's Just
waiting to Kill me, and all who
appose'v. Will we ever see a
Black president? Likely, Sounds
Hevensent. I wouldn't Bet on it.
and stop going to are coutry aFrica
steeling gold & diamonds talking Bout
you helping people, we all Know thats
a Bunch of Bull. So to AmeickKKa,
I say stop Runing game ~~~~~~and
~~thinking~~ ~~~~~~ we Lame.

                    P.S

                a Black Voice.

- 138 -

Government

Please stop lying saying what you going to do because I see things from a different view

My neighborhood still messed up people still dying from drugs over run by thugs

White folks showing no love and it gets worse amerikkka I ain't scared of what

You killed my hero's just waiting to kill me and all who oppose you

Will we ever see a black president? Not likely sounds heaven sent I wouldn't bet on it

And stop going to our country Africa stealing gold and diamonds

Talking about you helping our people we all know that's a bunch of bullshit.

So to amerikkka I say stop running game and thinking we lame.

p.s. a black voice

My Hero   4 malcome X

you taught me to stand up for
what I belive in.
you taught me if I like something
I can aceive.
Buy any mean nessqry, to have a
vest ~~and a gun~~ an a gun is veay real.
Beware of thugs who annt scared
of blood or jail time, and never
do a crime you dont have to,
So for that I feel I have to
carry on tradition, carry the torch
and ~~████████~~ I Be wishing you was
still here to ~~led~~ lead us, But
Ima soildei, and suriver thru it all
I have stood tall in AmerickkKa's
twisted cruel white mans woeld,
and one day we shall really truely
overcome!

                              one Loue.

                    "Allah" Bless us all"

My hero

(4 Malcolm X)

You taught me to stand up for what I believe.
You taught me if I like something I can achieve.
By any means necessary
To have a vest and a gun is very real.
Beware of thugs, who aren't scared of blood or jail time,
And never do a crime you don't have too,
So for that I feel I have to carry on tradition,
Carry the torch and I be wishing you was still here,
To lead us, but I am a solider and a survivor thru it all
 I have stood tall in amerikkka's twisted cruel white man world,
One day we shall really truly overcome.
One love
"Allah bless us all"

what ever u do

All the Thugs, Pimps, Playa's, & hustlea's,
Niggas & Bitches office ~~dodes~~, ~~White niggas~~ dudes
too, Whatever yo shine is; Do what u
do. Just Stay tRue 2 u, an dont
Play gamES. Its all ABout the moNEY
That make everyBody gEtin Funny.
Dont Be No Dummy, Cuuse even Family
will cross you, taike It From mE
people(~~PEEPE~~ you thought was yo maN
a hundeed graNd JusT FoNEY.
FEmal ~~Bitches~~ you thought was DowN with
You is gowN (Just a DimE a dozen) Othew
they stgrt ~~Fucking~~ yo Cousin. I givE'Em
Straight "Thug LoviN" But Ima Chill

- 142 -

Whatever you do

All the thugs, pimps, playa's & hustler's nigga's and bitches

Office dudes white dudes too

Whatever your shine is

Do what you do just stay true to you

And don't play games. It's all about money that makes everybody act funny

Don't be any dummy cause even family will cross you

Take it from me people you thought was your man hundred grand just phony

Females you thought was down with is gone (just a dime a dozen)

Then they started doing your cousin

I give them straight thug loving
But I chill

'ERacism

You KEEP Coming Back, But I
gUESS you NeVeR lEft. You cause
So many LifeS & So many deaths.
So many years, so many teares
How much more do we have to
take? Should WE Just Sit around and
Let Fate Be Fate? Times have
changed But Not Really. SomE people
tRyE'd to eRase you. otHeRS tRyEd
to Chase you, How much longer
do we have to Face you?

Eracism

You keep coming back but, I guess you never left.

 You caused so many lives & so many deaths.

So many years. And so many tears.

How much more do we have to take? Should we just sit around and let fate be fate?

Times have changed but not really some people have tried to erase you.

Others tried to chase you.

How much longer do we have to face you?

Fallen Angel
(Hearts of men)

Did you hear the story about the Fallen Angel?
That Fell From heaven and got his Life in a tragel.
He tried to make it threw Life helping others,
but people took his Kindness For weakness making
him nothing, He did not Know, couldn't quiet understandy
how it was so much evil in the hearts of men,
he tried to comaside and come to turms that
this world could change, so many souls Lost it just
seems strange, But what can he do? He asked god and
was told only time will tell, He was very scared Living
his Life on A Living Hell, Did he Fell? is what he
kept asking him self, But all he can ~~keep doing~~ in
Life is LIVE In good health.

                    stay peaceful.

Fallen angel

Hearts of men

Did you hear the story about the fallen angel?

That fell from heaven and got his life in a tangle.

He tried to make it through life trying to help other but people took his kindness for weakness.

Making him nothing. He did not know, couldn't really understand.

How there was so much evil in the hearts of men.

He tried to come to terms that this world could change.

So many souls lost it just seem strange. But what can he do?

He asked god and he said only time will tell.

He was very scared living his life in a living hell.

But all he could do in life was live in good health.

Rebel

For those who Anit hear
my hero's, ~~alw~~ my piers
For that white Dude that follow
me in the store thinking I'm a
steel soming, its 2007 and people
still ~~Fronting~~. For Malcome
By any means with my gun iN
my palm. For Pac when its
War time ~~its~~ on! For you
suckers iN the White House we
gon paint it Gold, ~~and~~ 2 Represent
all the gold & money yall stole
From ARe contry. I am the
New eRa the New Malcome and
I dont smoke or tAke volumes.
You Dudes is twisted. Dont even
tAke your time sit Back it Listen.
While yall watch yall video's
chasing Females, YA game gon
stAil, Just got out of jail
you say you Learned your
Lesson I cant tell.

Rebel

For those who aren't here my hero's my peers.

For the white dude following me in the store thinking I'm going to steal something.

It's 2000 something and people is still fronting. For Malcolm x by any means with my gun in my   palm.

For Pac when its war times it's on. For you suckers in the white house we going to paint it

Gold to represent the gold and money yawl stole from our country.

I am the new era of Malcolm and I don't smoke or take volumes. You dudes are twisted
Don't even take your time just sit back and listen.
While yawl watching yawl video's chasing females yak game gone stale.
You just got out of jail
You say you learned your lesson I can't tell.

Soul & heart   det. a ~~████~~ & All y'all   everyBody
(you think you know?)

you wonder how I do this? How I stay on
top of my game, you wonder why I'm that
same ~~Rude~~ that never changed, I Know I'm
going through yo head Now and you got a
million g~~u~~estions, But Before you start asking
you NEED to Start trusting, IF you Read "Never
Understand me", you Can kind of glimse in my
Life, my own mama think I'm crazy, ~~I~~ I
Will Never Find a wife, and my Father, he
dont Know the half, he Been Locked up For
so many years my Life to him is Just a
shaft, I think Ima die old & Along, I
Bet you Like, God Damn! that ~~Rude~~ ~~Nigga~~ singing
that same old song, I Will never ForGet,
unless I Leave this Bitch an eRase my
pass all By myself Just Smoking that grass,
And I still Know, All the Fake ~~shit~~ that
you ~~Nigga's~~ People told.   Its cool.

"and if you Be leave   "I heard
the shit you heard   y'all opionions"
y'all don't Know me,
Know one does,
          only "Allah."

2003-████ Just E

Soul & heart dedicated too everybody

(Fuck all yawl pt. 2)

You wonder how I do this.

How I stay on top of my game you wonder why I'm that same dude who never changed.

I know I'm going through your head now and you got millions of questions

But before you start asking you need to start trusting,

If you read <u>never understand me</u> you can get a glimpse of my life

My own mama think I'm crazy and I will never find a wife and my father don't know the half

He's been locked up for so many years of my life to him is just a shaft.

I think i am going to die old and alone I bet you like god damn dude singing that same old song,

I will never forget, unless I leave this bitch an erase my past all by my self

Just smoking that grass and I still know the entire fake shit that you people told
It's cool.
And if you believe the shit you hear you don't know me no one does only Allah
I heard yawl opinions (da sequel)

Farewell Chicago (Living the Life) 98

① Bright city lights and the ~~Block~~ Block is
still hot, its cold out but we still clocking rocks
friends still coming, its money to. Be made
the jump out boys hit the block trying to get
paid. my girl stressing cause I ain't sexing but
Im hungry ass hell just two packs to go then
I made my meal for the day. so I catch the
"L" to the westside cause hey Im still broke
my nigga hit me on the pager like a Joe lets
smoke, so now I got a renson to ditch my bitch
we been fucking for 3 dayz straight my dick
tired of that shit. but she got a nigga back
and I love her for that she say she got
my baby, nothing above her for that and as a matter
of fact its still mob let no man separait what
we create and thats on me, that thug life
I been reparseting all my life and Im
tied can someone esle do it? no matter
where I go all I hear is C. Fluld.
from tattoo tears and scars to prison
jail bars to smoking drinking having having money
cians gave it all up for one nite
to see the ~~stars~~ stars,

Back to Bussiness

Farewell Chicago

(Living the life 98)

Bright city lights and the block is still hot its cold but we still clocking rocks fiends still coming

Its money to be made jump out boys hit the block trying to get paid.

My girl stressing because I'm not sexing but I'm hungry as hell just two packs to go

And I made my mail for the day. So I catch the L to the Westside because hey I'm still broke

My nigga hit me on my pager like a Joe lets smoke so now I got a reason to ditch my bitch

We had been fucking for three days straight my dick tired of that shit.

But she got a nigga back and I love her for that she say she got my baby nothing above her

For that and as a matter of fact it's still mob let no man separate what we create and

That's on me that thug life I been representing all my life and I'm tired can someone else do it?

No matter where I go all I hear is c fluid. From tattoo tears and scares to prison jail
Bars smoking drinking having cars having things I gave it all up for night to see the stars
Back to business

If only it was real

If only it was true, she say she "Love" me I wish I
knew How long has it Been Now and it still seem
Brand new, to much D.V shit ~~Fucking~~ Messing wit you they
gone see me on t.V going out Like that, to much
drama. Is it worth it? How much more worse
can a curse get? But we was meant to
Be thats what they say. But who is they? is
They going to Jail? is they smoking crack? maybe
They is, maybe they Need to mind they biss:
maybe they Need to Raise they own kids. Im ~~tied~~
maybe they Need to Leave us along Im tied
of that same song, you know ~~that song~~ here we go
again. Preying For my downfall But in Reailty
I ~~win~~ Just so you know, anit yall tied
of six years of Being Broke? Loves gonna get
Cha. is you a sucka For Love? Well I know
I was. But it wasnt Real maybe cause it didnt
make me Feel,,, maybe the spark wasn't there
maybe it was the bed and the Liquor, maybe
~~it was~~ my Dick getting Bigger, maybe it
was Really trust that wee Lacked but I
know what it wasnt,,, Black!!

If only it was real

(4 someone)

If only it was true she says she in love with me

I wish I knew how long has it been now and it stills seems brand new

Too much dv shit messing with you they going to see me on TV going out like that.

Too much drama is it worth it? How much worse can a curse get?

But we were meant to be that's what they say.

But who is they?

Are they going to jail? Is they smoking crack?

Maybe they is maybe they need to mind there business

Maybe they need to raise their own kids

Maybe they need to leave us alone I'm tired of hearing that same old song.

You know that song here we go again, praying for my downfall but in reality

I win just so you know, aren't yawl tired of six years of being broke?

Loves going to get cha. Are you a sucker for love?

Well I know I was but it wasn't real maybe because it didn't make me feel...

Maybe the sparks wasn't there maybe it was the bud and the liquor.

Maybe it was the dick getting bigger maybe it's really trust that we lacked

But I know what it wasn't... black!!!

Take my eyes

4 my son

So you may C the World, TAKE my eyes
So you can see your girl, TAKE my eyes
So you may Live your Life, TAKE my eyes
To MAKE things right, I have seen so much
PAiN and greif I would Rather Be Blind to
Let one of mine Be, Im 30 this year
KNow more of that For me so take my eyes
and go to college and get some knw.

Take my eyes

(4 my son)

So you may see the world take my eyes so you can see your girl

Take my eyes so may live your life

Take my eyes pain and grief I'd rather be blind than let one of mine be

I'm 30 this year so no more of that for me so

Take my eyes and go to college and get some thing.

one night (one wish)

if I could have one night wit you
I promise Baby I would make it right
with you, Candle Light Dinner plus Remy on
the rocks all Night wit you Dont worry
Baby I wont ~~Bite~~ ~~oo~~ you I' rather take you
to the club and Party all Night with you
I ~~oo~~ Visionize the day ~~seeing~~ you naked
Dark Brown skin hips and ~~oo~~ thy's Baby
Check it I know you see it to cause you
mois in Between I see the way you
~~stan~~ Stair you Be like why why you Looking
so mean, I reply its the thug in me may not
seem like it But ~~I got~~ alot of Love in me. That
you can have For one night then go back
your BabyFather and Be' like Damn Im Not
Filling Right, Never to Be told only sold I
Been in this game since I was Fiftteen years
~~old~~ game Never Lame, Baby call me two
Cold its Really Not a game ~~oo~~ you just two
old and ~~latre~~

2 Nice, and soso Wonderfull

so Right

One night

(one wish)

If I could have one night with you I promise baby I would make it right with you

Candle light dinner with Remy on the rocks. All night with you but don't worry I won't bite you,

You rather I take you to the club and party all night with you I envisioned the day

I see you naked dark brown skin hips and thighs baby check it

I know you see it to cause your moist in between I see the way you stare like

Why, why, why you look so mean I reply it the thug in me may not seem like it

But I got a lot of love in me that you can have for one night then go back

To your baby father like damn I'm not feeling right never to be told only sold

I've been in this game since I was fifteen years old game never lame
Baby call me to cold it's really not a game you just too old and to late
2 nice and so, so wonderful
So right

When I die (my demise)

When I die; at my Furaral dont
even Cry For me, Dont smile
Fown nothing, Just Look; Look
at the young nigga yall hated
for so many years, the nigga yall
tryed to Be, the nigga yall envyed
wishing I died along tome ago. I
was way ahead of my time, I
Live thru my unBorn Kids, this is
Gods plan Not mine. No more stress
Im finally Free Kicking it with
pac 3 malcome they welcomed me.

When I die

(my demise)

When I die at my funeral don't even cry for me don't smile or frown nothing just look,

Look at the young nigga yawl hated for so many years the nigga

Yawl tried to be the nigga yawl envied wishing I died a long time ago

I was way ahead of my time I lived thru unborn kids this gods plan not mine

No more stress I'm finally free kicking it with Pac and Malcolm

They welcomed me

Thug Heart (I Was Born in this Thug Life)

everything you see is me From the Shoes to the
clothes to getting Money to Sexing hoe's I been Doing since
"93, I grew to Be a "G" had to earn my Stripes, still
taking yo Lady if you aint Sexin her Right. Too nights
the Night Like Betty Wright to get it popping. Nigga's
turn sqaures I see alot of Flag dropping. These
Streets is real Now In dayz you will get that ass
killed trya Be real. Shit the real aint even Real
we all Thugs through its still love Joe thats
What they say. But every Nite I know I'm Not
the only one that Pray. Day in and Day out Sun up
to Sunday, I Just WANTA Live in chill good
to I'm grey, with a half of Mill Not tell me
how that F Mil Sound good Dont it, But some of
you prolly wont make it to get a crazy check
Before they come take it yo Life. So Dont
Be stupid Joe cause when you waste it, you
know, and I Not trya kick Nothing in you earn
You aint heard, I Just speak the Real I wrote
words, my ghetto Life style in the Form of
poems. I'm to Thugged out But my heart is
harm, my Last Words to you Playa's
and misses Betta Keep it tight AN stack
yo Riches,

on Be Broke!!

Thug heart

(I was born in this thug life)

Everything you see is me from the shoes to the clothes to getting money to

Sexing hoe's I have been doing since 93. I grew to be a G had to earn my stripes

Still taking your lady if you aren't sexing her right. Too nights the night like Betty wright

To get it popping niggas turn squares I see a lot of flag dropping. These streets is real now

In days you will get that ass killed trying to be real. Shit the real aren't even real we all thugs

Though its still love Joe that's what they say. But every night I know I'm not the only who pray.

Day in and day out sun up to Sunday I just want a live and chill good to I'm grey.

With a half a mill now tell me how that feel, sounds good don't it but some of you

Probably won't make it to get a crazy check before they come take it your life.

So don't be stupid Joe cause when you waste it you know and I not trying to kick

Nothing in your ear you have not already heard, I just speak the real I write words my ghetto life style

In the forms of poems I'm to thugged out but my heart is warm. My last words to you playa's &
Misses better keep it tight and stack. Your riches............   or be broke.

Revolutionary Warfare Pt. 1.

Rule one strategy tactics techniques Look dumb
But I ~~see~~ they Soft to Fuck all them, Gotta Bust only
if necessary. Nigga a vest is very necessary
if Niggas carrying heavy metal, Beware of thugs
who ain't scared of Blood or Jail time. That's why
my young niggas pack heavy nines, The Beauty of Life.
was when my mom said nigga you could be christ
I wasn't old enough to hold my dick and pee
Right Jesus what is he like? I picture him
standing with diamonds on him Little different
from the way my momma saw him, Practice
you aiming, Physical Training Your
endurance, gotta keep your Stamina banging
What we Learned in school Teaching smart
ways to kill I'm thinking Ghandi was a
fool But Buds the fool got me thinking
out loud, think its Sweet
I'll Blow your Brains out,

Revolutionary warfare

Pt1

Rule one strategy tactics techniques look dumb but I see they soft so fuck
all them

Got to bust only if necessary nigga vest is necessary if niggas carry heavy
metal beware of thugs

Who aren't scared of blood or jail time. That's why my young niggas pack
heavy nines

The beauty of life was when my mom said nigga you could be Christ

I wasn't even old enough to hold my own dick and pee right Jesus what is he
like I picture him   standing with diamonds on him

Little different from the way my momma saw him practice you aiming

Physical training your endurance got to keep your stamina banging what we
learned in school teaching smart ways to kill

I'm thinking Ghandi was a fool but buds the fool got me thinking out loud

Think its sweet i blow your brains out.

Revolutionary Warfare pt.2

My revolution is as real as Bobby Seale's I build
with dudes in a ribs worth a quarter mill in
dix hills, for Fish Scales: To cop guns, when the
time come I'll mask up and get my comrades off the
Bus Fuck the Beef I'll snatch your seeds from
Chuckie Cheese and Feed Them to the rats in
the Back of the P's Black Fatigues and Black Boots
on the sofa, Black hoopie Black Vitton holsters
my motions dont appear to repel at divisions
my pops did strong For 22 long Years in prison
Fuck the system Im like a modern day Hitler
Black gorilla, crip and Blood in one nigga
My nigga Know Im straight I Beat a case
For Bushh at police, nigga the name E
its the new Black movement, the street revolution
22 gun salute the new Huey Newton

Revolutionary warfare

Pt2

My revolution is as real as Bobby Seale's I build with dudes in cribs worth a quarter mills

In Dix hills for fish scales to cop guns when the time comes ill mask up and get my comrades'

Off the bus fuck the beef ill snatch your seeds from chucky cheese and feed them to the rats

In the back of p's I'm black fatigues and black boots on the sofa black hooptie

Black Viton holster my motions don't appeal to repel divisions my pops did strong for 22 long years in prison fuck the system I'm like a modern day Hitler black gorilla Crip and blood

In one nigga my niggas know I'm straight I beat a case for busting at the police

Nigga the name E it's the new black movement, the street revolution 22 gun salutes

The new Huey newton.

Revolutionary Warfare pt 3

Teach your women how to hold the
Family down In case something happens
to us. Fathers, Protect your kids grab
Revolvers The women plays part of our
life Force, What we Fight For. My heart
goes to you Beautiful wife in war.
Listen more talk less, Watch all But trust
none demand your Respect. and Be Ready
to die. What you Believe in. And Ride
all the time Not just when Convenient
Justice and Freedom, wisdom and understanding
we the lost children of Africa In this
Western world Region You ain't a man you
coward if you cant support the girl you
put a seed in. Strong Rule the weak, The
wise Rule the strong. When its war time
think Before getting it on. stay prepared
Cover your track. I don't care when its
on its on in Revolutionary Warfare.

Revolutionary warfare

Pt3

Teach your women how to hold the family down in case something happens to us

Fathers protect your kids grab revolvers the women plays part of our life force

What we fight for my heart goes to you beautiful wife in war listen more talk less

watch all but trust none demand your respect and be ready to die for what you believe in and ride all the time not just when

Convenient justice and freedom wisdom and understanding we lost the children of Africa

In this western world region you not a man you coward

If you can't support the girl you put a seed in. strong rule the weak

The wise rule the strong when its war time think before you get it on.

Stays prepared and cover your tracks

I don't care when it's on it's on in revolutionary warfare.

<u>I'm still Around - 2 ex thats still alive</u>

Naw Nigga u anit Dreamin its true the Lil Nigga you once
Knew is still here. Been A Long road But I hold my OWN
dudes talk Real Greasy on these cellar phones I Laugh and
blow it off Leave it along; meanwhile since 2000 I been
on my own. No girl No kids Just a Cellar phone.
Not really a place to Call my OWN. and Im Loving
it. Its Just me so Im Dubbing it, I do Not Know
how people Live in a One room shack I
got to get paid since I Learned how To Cook
crack. That shit was Easy. Had these Females coming
In Flocks cheesing me. You seen the pictures.
Thats game. In time I got Bigger Real quicker.
Females came and went after they Money
was spent, I smoke alot of Blunts But my mind
stay Intent; I mean on track cant Loose count
when I counting them stacks. I got these Fake niggas coming
In packs trying to Be Down I got these white folks
that smile in my Face then turn they head in Town,
But I Dont care as Long I got them the N's is there
then Im a Blow this town, then its Back to the Block
to plot another town. Call that the take over. I
move in silece, I like that quiet money real quiet,
I know them people's is watching they Loving me
Clocking that south side shit Nigga stop it, I Love the
hustle Love the game Love how I make niggas
Look So Lame Better wake up you
squares. Poping all that shit in the club But
yull Some playa. Ha!!

You Niggas Lames in the Brain
wit No game

Still around

(2 ex that's still alive)

Now nigga u is not dreaming it's true the little nigga that you once knew is
still here
Been a long road but I hold my own dudes talk real greasy on these cellular
phones
I laugh and leave it along meanwhile since 2000 I've been on my own no
girl any kids
Just a cellular phone Not really a place to call my own And I'm loving it it's
just me
So I'm dubbing it I don't know how people live in a one room shack I got
to get paid
Ever since I learned how to cook crack that shit was easy
I had these females coming in flocks cheesing me
You've seen the pictures that's game in time I got bigger real quicker
Females came and went after they money was spent I smoked a lot of blunts
but my mind intent
I mean on track cant loose count when I'm counting them stacks.
I got these fake niggas coming in packs trying to be down
I got these white folks in my face smiling then they turn their heads and
frown
But I don't care as long as I got them the n's is there then it's back to the block
to plot another town
Call that the takeover I move in silence I like that quiet money real quiet I
know them peoples is watching they loving me clocking that Southside shit
nigga stop it
I love the hustle I love the game love how I make niggas look lame
Better wake up you squares popping all that shit in the club but yawl some
playas ha!!
You niggas is lame in the brain with no game.

My "Ghetto Quran"

Chicago 91,   my "Ghetto Quaran"

When you the talk of the Southside you the talk of the
Day see Niggas Feared E an Respected C For all you
Slow Muthafucka's Im Break it Down Cleaner see C
was the Bussiness and E was the Killer Remember
He use to push that old school shit that Said It
get you Sea Sick I Just Set Back an peep
Shit, Smoking mad Joints and shit and staying
Blunted had the Whole hood working For E For $5.00
as a yownth all I even Did Was Sell Crack
I Use to Look up to niggas hurt me in my heart too
here that Nigga Snicth Like that how HE go out
Like that Rumurs In the hood was Just For Snicthn
I anit Believe that shit he help get my First Few
Kicks, I had the Jordans, max's, one's and the threes
he use to drive his truck threw sitting on them
thangs and Being wise I got all Names of guys
Who Deathit wit pie's Like tree and Law I Swear
to God them the hardest Niggas I ever saw.
I Remember Lord Got Stabbed In the neck
By a Bitch he was thya hit Then told his
connect some nigg Robbed him For three Jabs
thats all was sAid next thing you know
niggas was dead.

"My ghetto Quran"

(1991 Chicago)

When you talk of the south side you the talk of the day see niggas feared E

And respected c for all you slow muthafucka's I'm going to break it down clearer see

C was the business and E was the killer remember he used to push that old school shit

That said it get you sea sick I just set back an peeped shit, smoking mad joints and

Shit staying blunted had the whole hood working for E for $500 as a youth all I ever did

Was sell crack I used to look up to niggas hurt me in my heart to hear that nigga snitched,

Like that l how he got out like that rumor in the hood was just for snitching

I didn't believe that shit he helped me get my first few kicks I had the Jordan's max's one's

And the threes he used to drive his truck thru the hood, sitting on them thangs and being wise

I got all the names of guys that dealt with pies. Like tree and law I swear to god

Them the hardest niggas I ever saw. I remember lord got stabbed in the neck by a bitch

He was trying to hit then told his connect some niggas robbed him for three jabs that was all that was said.

Next thing you know niggas was dead.

That First shit is a dose of some shit that Im on
Consiter the Second Chapter in the my Ghetto Quaran
I know a lot of Niggss stacking dou Like
Mario He walk up in down the Block wit a hole in
his Nose threw out my struggle's in the
ho'od I started Learning Lifes I Bitch with a
Pretty Face But she burning. I Wanna Get
Cash then dash an Run threw money like
Its Nothing spend n's all the the time Like C man
po pimp and shot Gunn they in the Feds now
they know what they Facing 200 years Wit
and Killers like timbo! Round here Shook Niggss
Fuck they keep it in motion come around with your
masons Jewels you can get Robbed Like Ocean
Lord Knows Dondy had Lost his soul I talking
Ferri drops wit Lusy Vaton Interar might sound
like Im Bullshiting But Nigga Im For Real
But Dondy was No Dummy got People to wash
the money and than lem got Ks so the Feds
started chasing Feds couldnt ck
get em Dirty So settle k
For tax. Invation.

The second chapter in my ghetto Quran

That first shit is a dose of some shit that I'm on nigga this the second chapter in my ghetto Quran

I know a lot of niggas stacking dough like Mario he walks up and down the block

With a hole in his nose threw out my struggles in the hood I started learning life's a bitch

With a pretty face but she burning I want to get cash then dash and run through money

Like it nothing spend n's all the time like c man po' pimp and shot Gunn they in the feds

Now they know what the facing 200 years with killers like timbo and fuck masons round here

Shook niggas they keep it in motion come around with your jewels you will get robbed like ocean lord knows Donnie had lost his soul

I talking 745's with luey Vitton interior might sound like I'm bullshitting but nigga

I'm for real but Donnie was no dummy got people to wash the money and then

The mob got knocked so the feds started chasing fed's couldn't get him dirty so

Settled for tax invasion.

a T.I.P to Cheif June money what one was about · Joe
Prince had Cream Im talking crazy cream like
South pole All my life I heard story about Jamanicans,
Down South   Niggas getting like us, alot of Niggas
like ME But they Been In the   hood all they like
And Dont KNow who I KNow Writings poEms is
the Best way I expose how I Feel, If I ain't
Rich By 36 Im Be dead or In Jail, Coming Up
I heard driking to much · Boy WEll Leave you confused
and If you watch the New you'll see playas in
this game to Loose, but Not ME Im staying
sucka Free Like '93 Fuck a Bitch and a Nigga
You can miss me With that Bullshit I told Niggas
Last year next is the Cash year · We all
Clear everybody here REConize the game spitting
in your   ear.

        So its Understood

A tip. to Chief June money

What he was about Joe lord had cream I'm talking crazy cream like South
Pole

All my life I heard stories about Jamaican's down south nigga getting like
us a lot of nigga's

Like me but they been in the hood all they life and don't know who I know
writing poems

is the best way I express how I feel if I'm not rich by thirty six I'll be dead
or in jail coming up

I heard drinking too much boos well leave you confused and if you watched
the new

You'll see playas in the game to loose but not me I'm staying sucker free like
93 fuck a bitch and a nigga you can miss me

With that bullshit I told niggas last year next is the cash year we all clear
everyone here

Recognize the game spitting in your ear.

So it's understood

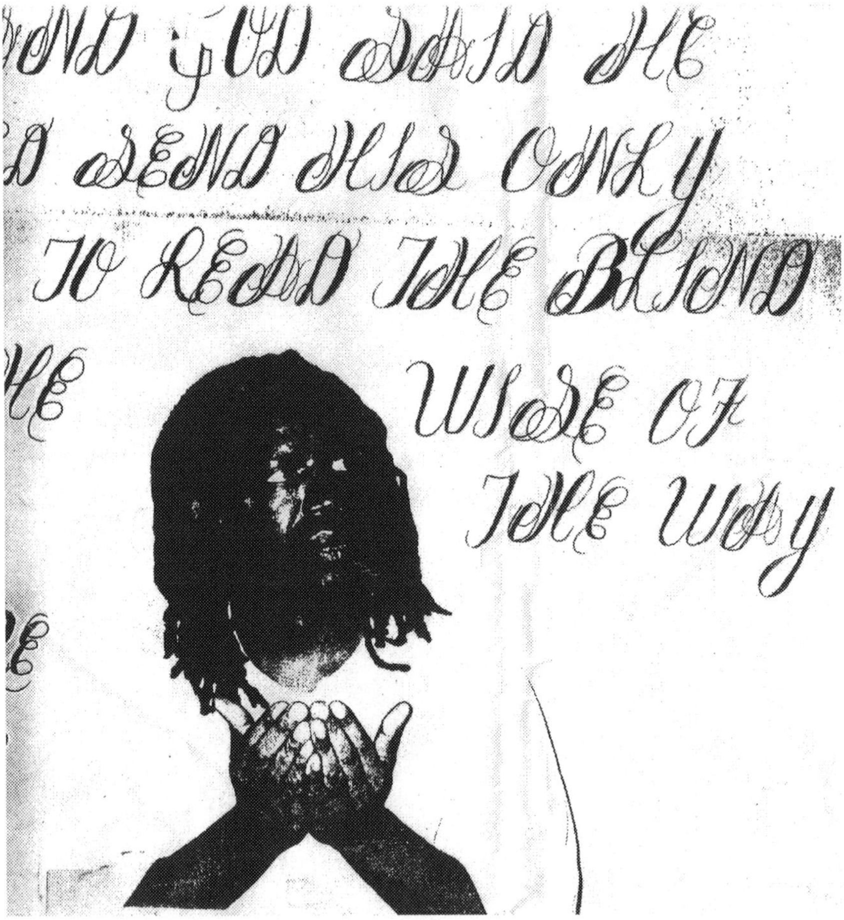

GOD SAID HE
SEND HIS ONLY
TO READ THE BLIND
WISE OF
THE WAY

The Lost Poems Of E.X. My Father

I AM THE ONE

THE BLACK JESUS IN THIS DAY AND TIME - TELLING YOU
NOT TO DO DOPE - NOT TO EAT THE SWINE. I AM ADAM WITH
MORE THAN ONE EVE - MY DEFINITION OF MARRIAGE YOU WOULD
NEVER BELIEVE.

I AM TRUTH NEVER FALLING FOR LIES - A SOUL SEARCHER RIGHT
BEFORE YOUR EYES. A RELEGION THATS REAL - AND EASY TO
UNDERSTAND - I AM LOVE TO A FEMALE AND WISDOM TO A MAN.
I AM REBORN WITH A LIGHT - THAT WORKS IN ANY DARK - SORT
OF LIKE NOAH AFTER THE STORM - STEPPING OFF THE ARK.
EVEN BEFORE MY BIRTH - I COULD NEVER HAVE BEEN A SOILDER -
WITH SOME FAKE COMMANDER LOOKING OVER MY SHOULDER. I MIGHT
HAVE BEEN A WARRIOR - I KNOW I WAS A LEADER IN SOME OTHER
TIME - I HAVE A VISION - I AM NOT BLIND.

I AM A INTIRE UNIVERSE POINTING AT THE SUN - BACK ON EARTH
I AM THE ONLY TRUE DON. I AM MALCOLM X, DR. KING AND
MINISTER FARRAKHAN ALL ROLLED UP IN ONE - A SCIENCETIST
A PREACHER - A MASTER MIND DON. I'LL ALWAYS BE MORE THAN MEETS
YOUR EYE - LIKE A NEWBORN BABY TAKING HIS FIRST CRY. BUT
YOU CAN'T CHANGE ME - SHOULD YOU FEED ME - WASH ME - I AM SO SO CLEAN -
THE WAY I FELL INSIDE SOMETIMES MAKE ME LOOK MEAN.

I AM WHAT I AM - AND THATS ALL
THAT I AM -
THE LIVING!

I am the one

The black Jesus in the day and time
Telling you not to do dope not to eat swine
I am Adam with more than one eve
My definition of marriage you would never believe
I am truth never falling for lies
A soul searcher right before your eyes
A religion that real and easy to understand I am love to a female and wisdom
to a man
I am reborn with a light that works in the dark
Sort of like Noah after the storm stepping out of the ark
Even before my birth I could have never been a solider
With some fake commander looking over my shoulder I might have been a
warrior
I know I was a leader in some other time I have a vision I am not blind
I am an entire universe pointing at the sun back on earth I am the only true
don
I am Malcolm x, Dr. King and minister Farrakhan all rolled in one a
scientist
A preacher a masterminds son, I'll always be more than meets your eye
Like a new born baby taking his first cry but you can change me
Should you feed me wash me I am so clean
The way I feel inside sometimes makes me look mean.
I am what I am and that's all I am. The living
E.X.

"Falling in a Dream"

I reach out my hand, but knowbodys there "But yet the faces are smiles of care. The voices are loud as if they want me to hear, they're having a good time with joy and cheer. I'm screaming out for rope to pull me back up, but knowone can see me as they turn up their cups. I smell the wine and the weed and sex in the air, I hear gun shots and tires screaming, is anyone up there. I fall to the bottom and the sounds go away" Its cold down here "But I'll live to see a brighter day.

"O.k. I'm awake"

Here about my riches when I enter into the world" "Everyday of the week brothers cuffing them girls" Thats my click doing what they do, Top-Son is the name, P.I.M.P. too. My heart has holes in it, making my blood re-created and its getting cold. And I pray to the father to save my soul. If you could borrow my mind and see what I see, you'll understand why the fakes depart, and the real, chill with me. I chase cabbage like a rabbit who is hungry all the time, get what you can get - cause I'm coming for mines.

Falling in a dream

I reach out my hand but know bodies there but yet the faces are smiles of care
The voices are loud as if they want me to hear there having a good time
With joy and cheers I'm screaming out for the rope to pull me back up,
But no one can see me as they turn up there cups.
I smell the wine and the weed and the sex in the air, I hear gun shot and
tires screaming
Is anyone up there I fall to the bottom and the sound go away its cold down here
But I'll have to live to see a brighter day.
"Okay I'm awake"
Here about my riches when I enter into my world every day of the week
Brothers cuffing them girls that is my click doing what they do top sons are
the name, P.I.M.P. too.
My heart has holes in it making my blood recreated and it's getting cold.
And I pray to the father to save my soul. If you could borrow my mind and
see what I see,
You'll understand why the fake depart and the real chill with me.
I chase cabbage like a rabbit that is hungry all the time, get what you can get
Cause I'm coming for mines.

So marvelous - So so real - So nice with the game - And
the sex is magical - Always putting out there flame-
Then I start my own fire - Shooting sparks straight to her
mind - I treat her so gentle - I treat her so kind - Learning
from her all the things she adore - Introducing her to a
part of her she never knew before -

That part of her is me - She have two eyes but yet she
cannot see - Once again I am on top on my spill - She start
telling me what she want do - But I know that she will -
My timing must be perfect as I prepare for the THEFT - 'Couf
I steal her heart and keeps it for myself - Not willing to
share it with anyone - Not even with her - I mean I'll let
her borrows it - To go buy me a fur -

Or better yet something with a big bling - Having her singing
the words of Sade (Your love is king). No certain color - Black
Red - Yellow - White - They all say the same thing - I am always
right - I let them go - For more reasons than one - Most of
the time to see them have fun - Using my skill on so many
games - Without even knowing that they are running my game -

There are only so many hearts that my milk can hold - And
in this game - my blood will always be cold - Like ice is frozen
So real - So so nice -
                    The Living EM

So marvelous

I still steal

So marvelous- so real – so nice with the game- and the sex is magical-always putting out there flame-then start my own fire- shooting sparks straight to her mind- I treat her so gentle I treat her so kind- learning from her all the things she adores- introducing her to a part of her that she never knew before.

That part of her is me- she has two eyes but yet she cannot see- once again I am on top on my spill- she starts telling me what she won't do but I know she will- my timing must be perfect as I prepare for the theft-'boof' I steal her heart and keep it for my self- not willing to share it with anyone not even with her- I mean I'll let her borrow it to go buy me a fur.

Or better yet something with a big bling having her singing the words of Sade (your love is king)

No certain color black red yellow white they all say the same thing I am always right I let them go for more reasons than one most of the time to see them have fun using my skills on so many lames without even know they're running my game.

There are only so many hearts that my mind can hold and in this game my blood will always be cold like ice so frozen so real so-so nice.

The living E.X.

STOP LOOKING AT ME.
WHEN I PUT ON THE LEATHER COAT WITH THE KANGO ON
YOU WATCHING ME LIKE I'M UP TO KNOW GOOD - AND I'M SOON
TO DO WRONG - AND WHAT ABOUT THE WHITE MINK - WITH
THE SILK SUIT - NOW YOU AND YOUR GIRL FRIENDS ALL
IN MY FACE TRYING TO GET MY LOOT - I JUMP IN MY
STREET SLAVE GEAR WITH THAT HUSTLING STYLE LOOK -
THIS SOME NEW SHIT - SO I GOT YOU ALL SHOOK -

MAKE ME GO HOME AND PUT THEM FOTI' ON - SHARP AS
A TAC WITH MY CELLUM PHONE - NO CALL IN - I JUST CALL
OUT - AND I GOT NO TIME TO DISCUSS WHAT I'M ABOUT - I
PUT THAT LONG BLACK COAT ON WITH NOTHING BUT BLACK
ON TO MATCH - WHEN YOU SEE ME LIKE THIS - YOU'LL LOWER
ALL THE STRETCH - IF GOD IS WITH YOU - YOU'LL SEE ANOTHER
DAY - CAUSE IT GETS REAL UGLY WHEN I DRESS THAT WAY -

ALL STYLES IN DRESSING - YOU MIGHT EVEN SEE ME IN ALL
WHITE - TALKING TO A GROWN ON THE CORNER - SHINING THOUGHTS
OF LIGHT - LIKE BISHOP MAGIC DON IN THAT GREEN AND GOLD
WITH A UNUSUAL CONVERSATION TO STEAL YOUR UNSEEN SOUL - THE
SAME AFFECT WHEN I JUMP IN A PUSSY PINK SUIT - THEY COME
FROM ALL DIRECTIONS - YOU THINK I GIVE A HOOT -
BELIEVE IT OR NOT - BUT I WOULD FOREVER BE FREE - IF YOU
FAKE - HATING BROTHERS - STOP LOOKING AT ME -

The Living E.Z

Stop looking at me

When I put on the leather coat with the kanga on you watch me like I'm up to no good and soon to do no wrong and what about the white mink with the silk suit now you and your girlfriends all in my face trying to get my loot I jump in my street slave gear with that hustling style look this some new shit so I got you all shook.

Make me go home and put them forte's on sharp as tact with my cellular phone no call in I just call out and I got no time to discuss what I am bout. I put on that long black coat on with nothing but black on to match when you see me like this you lower all the scratch. If god is with you you'll see another day because it gets real ugly when I dress this way.

All styles in dressing you might even see me in all white talking to a group of sons on the corner shining through the light like bishop don Juan in that green and gold with a simulant conversation to steal your sister soul. The same affect when I jump in a pussy pimp suit they come from all directions you think I give a hoot.

Believe it or not but I will forever be free if you fake hating brothers stop looking at me
The living E.X.

Its Just A Poem!

If it is written, then let it be done, If you go against
The writing, then its you that ends up with none. I am who
I say I am, I don't lie, cry, I am the after life - I will never
Die. From the earth to the sun, its 93,000,000 miles, my
Knowledge is emacating, Just like my style. No happiness, no
Saddness, No regrets, You think you know me, You haven't
even seen me yet. My love is action, which know words can
truly Describe, You'll never get the full effect unless you
stand strong by my side.

You aint got nothing, Scared to get something, Cause you are
use to nothing, You think you have something - Because you never
Had nothing, So something seems like something; But your something
is nothing, You can't get something if you don't know what
something is. Now ask yourself, what is your something. Its
Nothing.

Playing with me as if I am a toy - Sharing my thoughts with
The girl, with the boy. Why o why do you look for misunderstanding
Is it because I am 2 demanding.

"Joz Son"
1931

It's just a poem!

If it is written then let it be done if you go against the writing then it's you
that ends up with none.
I am who I say I am I don't lie cry I am after life. I will never die.
From the earth to the sun its 93,000,000 miles my knowledge is emacalint.
Just like my style no madness no sadness no regret you think you know me
You haven't even seen me yet my love is action which no words can truly describe
You'll never get the full effect unless you stand by my side.

You don't got nothing scared to get something because you are use to nothing
you think
You have something because you never had anything so something seems
like something
But your something is nothing you can't get something if you don't know
what something is.
Now ask yourself what is your something it's nothing

Playing with me as if I am toy sharing my thoughts with the girl, with the
boy. Why oh why do
You look misunderstood is it because I am to demanding?
"Top Sons" (1937)

Street Prisoner

Look at your motherfucking neighborhood dogs - Fake
ass preachers eating that hog - Drunks standing on the
corner begging for a dime in order to buy a bottle of wine.
It's a blood sucking church and a devil liquor store on every
other street - And your stupid ass is selling poison and
carrying the heat aimming at your brother - But ends
up shotting a lil girl - Now you lock down calling
mama to make bail.

When your trick ass was out there - you gave nothing to
moms - Listening to the big words in the court room - Just
realizing that you are dumb. Asking that serious devil
sitting next to you - What does it mean - Life in prison
no less than twenty two - Now you remember that
fine ass sister that you tryed to kill for - you left
her a benz. - A house and none of the kidds is yours.

What happen to the brother that you was trying to kill
He is laying up with your girl - living off of your
will - Ok you tough - stupid bastard) - Whats your next
move - you think about hanging up but that aint cool
She told you to stop calling - So now the number has change
Send your sister to set up a visit with him - but that can't
be arrange - Now you wishing that the baby girl was
your lil daughter - The game is over - Don't insert another
quater.

The Living Evil

Street prisoner

Look at your mother fucking neighborhood dog. Fake ass preachers eating that hog Drunks standing on that corner begging for a dime in order to buy a bottle of wine

It's a blood sucking church and a devils liquor store on every other street. And you're stupid ass is selling poison and carrying the heat. Aiming at your brother but end up shooting a little girl. Now you lock up calling mama to make bail.

When your tricks ass was out there you gave nothing to moms listening to the big words in the court room just realizing that you are dumb asking that serious devil sitting next to you what does it mean life in prison no less than twenty two? Now you remember that fine ass sister you tried to kill for. You left her a house bens and none of the kids are yours.

What happened to the brother that you was trying to kill he was lying up with your girl living off your will okay you tough stupid bastard what's your next move you thinking about hanging up but that isn't cool she told you to stop calling so now the number has changed.

Send your sister to set up a visit with her but that can't be arranged now you wishing that the baby girl was your little daughter the game is over don't insert another quarter

The living E.X.

The Scribble Scribe

~~All~~ All I
Fear is the thought of my childrens saying why Daddys not here.
From Romances to Finances - Making babies and taking chances - From
~~selling~~ selling drugs - Creating thugs - to having snap shots of
my mug. Police line up - sipping from fine cups - Never could get
enough. From Christian - to Moorish American - Muslim - The Nation
of Islam - Believe you me, I have did it all ~~and~~ Any Hing lots of fun

To many Faults To many mistakes - To many Females come on the
Takes - To many hand out - showing to much love - To much praying to
a Spirit up above. They say if you love someone set them free -
Then its safe to say that she was in love with me. Any female
that layed in my bed - I licked a few "But always got a head.
Still putting something on your mind - Still not eatting swine
Better yet - You can miss me with the meet - And don't think for
one minute that I dont eat. One Hundred and Ninety pounds and
Im Hungry all the time - I don't worrie about yours - So don't you
worrie about mines. You can take that hate - that weak fight game
you got and that ugly mean mug across the way - I got love - Im
good with my hands and Im in this game to stay. Perhaps you don't
understand what I said - let me break it down for the mentally
Dead. New game - New name - New school is exzactly what Im
saying - I make my own rules while you still delaying. Never
been a follower for more than a year - In control of my emotions
Especially my Fear. So Here Ye - Here Ye all across the land
If you think its not real - Then try your hand.

E. 8

The scribble scribe

All I fear is the thought of my children saying my daddy's not here from romances to finances making babies to taking chances from selling drugs creating thugs to having snap shots of my mug. Police lineup sipping from fine cups never could get enough. From Christian to Moorish American Muslim the nation of Islam believe you me I have did it all and had a lot of fun

Too many faults too many mistakes too many females come on the take to many handouts showing too much love too much praying to a spook above. They say if you love someone set them free then if it safe to say that she is in love with me. Any female that laid in my bed I licked a few but I always got a head still putting something on your mind still not eating swine.

Better yet you can miss me with the meat. And don't think for one minute that I don't eat. One hundred and ninthly pounds and I am hungry all the time. I don't worry about yours so don't worry about mine. You can take that hate that weak fight game you got and that ugly mean mug across the way. I got love I'm good with my hands and I'm in this game to stay.

Perhaps you don't understand what i said let me break it down for the mentally dead. New Game new name new school is exactly what I'm saying I make my own rules while you still delaying. Never been a follower for more than a year. In control of my emotion especially my fear.so hear ye hear ye all across the land if you think it's not real then try your hand.

E.X.

The REEN1

Once again I try to escape, by putting my thoughts in the head of somebody else faith. Everybody wants to be gansters, players, thats what they say. Am I the only one left in this world who understand how to pray. I want drink the whiskey I want drink the wine, and just because you have sight in your two eyes, it do not mean that you're not blind.

I want smoke your weed, I want take your pills, how can you do this drag and think that you are real. I want curse my elders - I want eat your meats - and for whom it may concern, I am straight from the streets. Keep eatting your chickens - keep eatting your steaks - and I'll be the last one eatting off the plate.

Jail on know jail, its been 41 years and I still am ahead of all of my peers. I don't hang around to wait on a chance I hit the grime and make everyone dance. I love the ladies but my lil family come first - money is like a day mouth - so I obey my thirst. I trust the people who put their trust in me, and thats the way it will always be.

Earl. K

No Weapon Formed against me shall prosper.

The Reeni

Once again I try to escape by putting my thoughts in the head of some ones else's faith. Everybody wants to be gangsters, players, that's what they say am I the only one left in this world who understands how I pray. I won't drink the whiskey I won't drink the wine and just because you have sight in your two eyes it doesn't mean that you're not blind.

I won't smoke your weed I won't take your pills how can you do this drag and think that you are real? I want curse my elders I won't eat your meats and for whom it may concern I am straight from the streets keep eating your chickens keep eating your steak and I'll be the last one eating of the plate.

Jail or no jail it's been 41 years and I still am ahead of all my peers I don't hang around to wait on a chance I hit the grime and make everyone dance. I love the ladies but my little family come first money is like a dry mouth so I obey my thirst. I trust the people who put their trust in me and that the way it will always be

No weapons formed against me shall prosper.

Earl X

EVERYBODY TALKING

EVERYBODY TALKING ABOUT THIS AND THAT - FAT CARS AND THOUSAND
DOLLAR STACKS. SOME SAY THEY ARE WITH ME UNTIL THE VERY END
CLAIMING TO BE FAMILY, MY GIRL AND CLOSE'S TO KIN. I SEND MORE
MALCOM X OUT TO THE WORLD THEN EVERYBODY SEND IN. EVERYBODY
GOT A STORY TO TELL - THIS IS WHERE MY STORY BEGIN.

EVERYBODY - ANYBODY - YOUR BODY - HIS AND HERS - THE WAY
YOU CHANGE YOUR SOCKS EACH TIME - THAT'S THE WAY I'LL CHANGE MY FUNS.
EITHER I WILL GO INTO THE FUTURE OR BACK IN TIME - EITHER
WAY - YOUR WIND WON'T STAND UP TO MINE. DON'T THINK IM SWEET
CAUSE LAST TIME I WAS OUT THERE I LET YOU EAT. THE SECOND TIME
AROUND IS ALWAYS BETTER THEN THE FIRST. BITCHE'S CANNOT DO NOTHING
BUT SUCK MY DICK AND OBEY THEIR THIRST.

EVERYBODY WILL BOW - YALL KNOW MY FREAKING PAST - THIS TIME I'LL
TRULY BE FREE AT LAST. NO WIFE & NO COMMITMENTS - NO LIVING
TOGETHER WITH NO HER - ME AND MALCOM X AND SOME TAILOR MADE CLOTHS.
GIVE ME MY 2 SONS AND LET MY 2 GIRLS YAH BACK AND WATCH THE
FAMILY BUSINESS AS THE MALCOM X STACK. ONE MORE TWO MORE
THREE - FOUR FIVE - ANOTHER NO LIMIT TO THE X - O' ITS
GOING TO BE LIVE

WHATS IN THE DARK MUST COME TO THE LIGHT   To: YOUNG"
WRONG IS WRONG AND RIGHT IS RIGHT   E.
GOOD NITE!

Your Dad. From E.X

Everybody's talking

Everybody's talking about this and that fat cars and thousand dollar stacks some say they are with me until the very end claiming to be family my girl and closest of kin. I send more Malcolm x out to the world then everybody send in everybody got a story to tell this is where my story begin.

Everybody anybody your body his and hers the way you change your socks each time that's the way ill change my furs either I will go into the future or go back in time either way your whip won't stand up to mine. Don't think I'm sweet because the last time I was out there I let you eat. The second time around is always better than the first. Bitches can't do nothing beside suck my dick and obey their thirst.

Everybody will bow Yawl know my freaking past. This time I will truly be free last. No wife-e no commitments no living together with no hoes me and Malcolm x and some tailored made clothes give me my two sons and let my two girls fall back and watch the family business as the Malcolm x stacks. one more two more three four five another no limit to the x oh' it's going to be live.

What's in the dark must come out to the light wrong is wrong right is right good night!

To young E from E.X.

I COME AS I AM.

BLACK JESUS ANSWER BACK! BELIEVE IN SOMETHING!
OR PERISH AS A FOOL!

1.) Where were you LAST night when I got jumped on?
I was standing by your side - making sure you made it home.

2.) Where were You when my home got stomped on?
I was making sure that it would only make him strong.

3.) Where were you when the police hit me with a bogus case, sprayed
mase in my face and took me to this place.?
I was riding with you to the bitter end - To teach you forgiveness
so that you would understand their sin

4.) Where were you when my mama was doing crack and we was
living in a one room shack? I was walking behind you son -
watching your back.

5.) Where were you when my father went to prison facing life?
I made him a sacrifice - so that you would be alright.

6. Where were you when my homie took that knife? I was
watching over you - so that you would have life.

7. Where were you when my grandmother died? I was assisting
the angels as they took her on her final ride.

8. When you were broke - gang hanging - starving and staging
I was preparing your father to guide you out of danger
BLACK JESUS - Forever - The Earth!

I come as I am

Young e talks to black Jesus

Black Jesus answers back believe in something or perish as a fool!

1. where were you last night when I got jumped on?

I was standing by your side- making sure you made it home.

2. where were you when my homey got stomped? I was making sure that it would only make him strong.

3. where were you when the police hit me with this bogus case sprayed mace in my face and took me to this place?

I was riding with you to the bitter end to teach you forgiveness, so that you would understand there sin.

4. where were you when my mama was doing crack and we was living in a one room shack?

I was walking behind you watching your back.

5. where were you when my father went to prison facing life?

I made him a sacrifice so that you would be alright.

6. where were you when homey took that knife?

I was watching over you- so that you would have a life.

7. Where were you when my grandmother died?

I was assisting the angel as they took her on her final ride.

8. Where were u when we were broke gangbanging, starving and slanging?

I was preparing your father to guide you out of danger

Black Jesus forever the truth!

And yes I did notice.
You trying to call me End one
time in greenbay. And I clear You
About that. Ha

I Didn't call my
father Dad until I came
Home in 91.
All of us called him Bro!

Lil Earl claim to be a outlaw - a outcast - maybe the accident
at eleven years old has damaged his mind. He say that our
relationship is based on cash - Now lets look at the definition of
A outcast - (A person who is rejected). By society)

Out-law - (a habitual criminal) if these 2 things fit you than I
guess thats who you are. When You was three years old - I came to jail
for home invasion. Before I came to jail - I use to sale custome Jewelry
And Bootleg things. In order to provide for you and your mother.
I use to keep you all the time back then - even when me and your
mother use to break up. And we use to break up a lot. The use to
go out and party and me and you would be at our first apartment
playing until you fall to sleep. You was about one year old back
then.
We went to the zoo a couple of times back then with your
Aunt Hazel. You was sort as milk. I could'nt even leave you
with your mother or you would start screaming - crying. When
even me and your mother took you to see your Kin folks. And
If I did not take my coat off - You would not take yours
off. The reason why I started doing crime is because my
hustle had played out - And my mother and father was making
to much money for me to get a job. At least Thats what All
Of the people told me when I tryed to get one.
I had a pety fowly - Thats why they would not let me Join
the army. That made crime a easy choice for me.

As long as you stay out of Jail
And Don't sale drugs - I'll always be proud of You So

Lil earl claim to be an outlaw

An outcast maybe the accident at 11 years old damaged his mind.
He say that our relationship is based on cash- now let's look at the definition of outcast: a person who is rejected by society.

Outlaw: a habitual criminal if these two things fit you then I guess that's who you are. When you was three years old –I came to jail for home invasion Before I came to jail I used to sell custom jewelry and bootleg things, in order to provide for you and your mother I used to keep you all the time back then. Even when I and your mom used to break up and we used to break up a lot. She used to go out and party and I and u would be at our first apartment playing until you fell asleep you were about one back then.

We went to the zoo a couple of times with your aunt hazel back then you were spoiled as milk. I couldn't even leave you with your mother or you would start screaming. Crying. Whenever me and your mama took you to see your kin folks and If I didn't take my coat off- you would not take yours off .the reason why I started doing crime is because my hustle had played out and my mother and father was making too much money for me to get a job at least that's what all the people told me when I tried to get one.

I had a petty felony that's why they wouldn't let me join the army. That made crime an easy choice for me.

As long as you stay out of jail

And don't sell drugs I'll always be proud of you son!

STAY ALIVE-

I want to tell you a l'l something about the life I live.
Behind these bars, this Jail shit is real. All I can do is
Pray and PLAN. Listening to my son growing into a man.
Working a Job for 40 hours a week. As they bring in more
Inmates bundle up like sheep. The annum wage for the month
is five dollars and 35 cent. They say the rest go toward
our food-lights and rent. Young brothers come in like 18 yrs
old with a natural life sentence, Man this shit is cold.
I pay for my phone calls- help my childrens in everyway I
can. They try to run me insane, do you understand what
I am saying. I try hard to keep in shape, to keep from fighting
a brother. I Rather stay peaceful and try to bump his
mother. I see a fake brother coming from a mile away, Don't
tell me not to call you a Nigga - I Just say what I say.
Rich Niggas - Big Niggas- Hoe Niggas too. I don't mean it
like the slave master do, cause I love all colors, black-e
gold too. They tell all type of stories about what they use
to do, Some claim to be bank robbers, Dope Dealers and big
Drug boys too. I listen to the stories half of the time
Some of them are real but most of them are lying.
I cut most of the outside world off -cause all they do
is lie, And I'm still wondering who at my mother funeral
didn't nobody cry. Everything that you are reading is all
facts and true. You got to be family to the ones who are
family to you. I live by my codes, my word, my rules
when you cross that line I do what I do. I respect everybody
and demand minds in return and with that bullshit
I am not concern. I won't go into the hustle even tho
its true, The game don't stop no matter what you do.
I leave you with a reminder that I am still in the
feds, But the fact still remains- I am alive -not dead.
How you!

                    C X

from the writing of

Still alive

I want to tell you a little something about the life I live. Behind these bars, this jail shit is real. All I
Can do is pray and plan. Listening to my son growing into a man, working a job for forty hours a
Week. As they bring in more inmate hurdle up like sheep. The minimum wage for the month is
Five dollars and twenty five cents. They say the rest goes toward our food, lights and rent.
Young brothers come in like eighteen years old with a natural life sentence, man this shit is cold.
I pray for my phone calls. Help my children's in every way I can. They try to run me insane do
You understand what I am saying. I try hard to keep in shape to keep from fighting a brother. I
Rather stay peaceful and try to bump his mother. I see a fake brother coming from a mile away.
Don't tell me not to call a nigga I just say what I say. Rich niggas big niggas hoe niggas too. I
Don't mean it like the slave master do, because I love all colors black-e-gold too. They tell all
Type of stories about what the used to do, some claim to be bank robbers dope dealers and big
Pimp boys too. I listen to the stories half the time some of them are real but most of them are
Lying. I cut most of the outside world off cause all they do is lie and still wondering why at my
Mother's funeral didn't know body cry. Everything that you are reading is a fact and true. You
Got to be family to the ones who are family to you. I live by my code my words my rules when
You cross that line I do what I do. I respect everybody and demand minds in return and with that
Bullshit I am not concerned. I want go into the hustle even doe its true, the game don't stop
No matter what you do. I leave you with a reminder that I am still in the feds, but the fact still
Remains I am alive not dead. How you!
From the writing of the munir letters.

E.X.

Love Notes & Pictures

Baby,

do u kno the feeling when u think you've known some1 ur whole life? I sorta feel that way bout you. I cant wait 2 live w/ u!

you make me feel amazing & I cant help falling 4 ur charm!

Everytime I'm w/ u, it feels so right.

I have fallen in love w/ you!

I know this might sound corny, but I think you might be the one I want 2 marry!

I have never felt this strong about someone. I'm glad I met you. I just wish I were 18 so I could live w/ you & my mom couldn't say nothing.

Question: If my mom kicks me out cn I come live w/ you?! Please?!

I love you!

always
- ur baby xoxo

Hey Baby -

My stomach hurts really bad! I
have really bad cramps today!
I am so stressed out right now!!

I came over yesterday - but you
weren't home - so I just went
home! I wanna be 18 NOW! I'm so
sick of people telling me wat to
do! also because I wanna be with
you & live with you! I LOVE YOU!

I just got a really bad headache!
anyways - I can't get you off my mind!
I can't stop thinking of you! I really
care about you and I love you so
much more!

Baby - I LOVE you so much! I can't wait
till I turn 18! we are gonna have so
much fun 2gether!

I miss you! I wanna leave skool
and come see you! I just hate
being away from you!

♥ always

- your baby girl
xoxo

To my love

I love you enuff to tell you this weather you think I'm lieing or not this is the truth.

For me to hit on my lady thats not me I'm sorry for that. It won't happen again.

For me to cut — part of ale are business partnas not happenin any more. your gonna have to trust me for once. & learn to trust me. hear me out.

I love you enuff to show you lot of respect. and bust my out trying to make things happen. Job feet.

Dirty

How about I suprise you with that ice cream in out freezer. lets do the math.

You + ICE cream = Me

~~and + ~~ ~~ = me~~

Eore gets ice cream rubbed all over hand stomach lichs it all up! emm emm good!

P.S.
Till Death do us part.

Love you forever

Stephanie

I'M SORRY FOR MY lyfe
Reasons of ashamement,
Pathethicness & Redemotion
Sharing THOUGHTS OF WHAT
WILL BE
I searched for MR WRIGHT & how
GLAD ID BE TO MaKe HIM PROUD OF
ME.....
KNOWING WHAT I KNOW NOW I ONLY
WOULDVE REPENTED FOR MY SINS
MRS. WRIGHT & ME COULD BE NOTHING
BUT UNTRU
SHE IS SHE & I AM I SHE IS BLACK & I AM
BROWN SHE IS WRIGHT & I AM WRONG
IF ONLY WE COME TOGETHER
PRAISE ALIJAH

Answer 2 all my Problems

Game says Belvi & Banana snapple
Look Niggah2 is Trippin
Day after Day It seems since i was
born, every Blessed Morning Down
on my Luck & my love im here to stay.

I DIDNT MEAN TO RUN AWAY, ONLY Allah
was there w/the creation of every baby
WE MADE. LA LA LA
     IM A WOMEN
YOUR QUEEN THE GODESS of my king
     WE GOT A SON
     WITH ONE MORE ANTERAZE ON THE WAY
I OWE you my lyfe H2 A WRAP
YOU MADE THAT CHOICE I NEVER SAID
THANK YOU, NEVER STAR STRUCK; JUST APRICCHVE
2 be what you called MINE. I'D DO WE-THANK
4 you the MAN who knows ME best
high in the $ DOWN ON My LUCK OR JUST
KEEPING IT REAL HE'S MY HEART MY SOUL
MY SPIRIT! REAL COVE.

Obtuse 2 me
Vary diff in many ways
As many would say want 2 planing,
Thy day we become one as a mate/mother
Husband + wife 2 be obviously
Obtuse 2 be is all we can be.
Love me 4 me, 4 that you will see
Fulfillment + happiness of our fam 2 be
acustom, E-Z Just love me 4 me
Truly yourz, Husband + wife, 2 be.

Marleeta
, Bart

- 215 -

Bonnie & Clyde Taking over Da World
Two dogz In A Pod, bonded by Real love,
Soon 2 B 2 Wrightz & no Wrongz, KING
& Queen 4Ever more   (Besides)
NOTHING MORE 2 DO: TAKE OVER DA WORLD
            GET MONEY
$$$$$ M O B $ $ $ $ $

        Marletta
            ♥S

            EARL
4Ever MORE TIL DEATH DO US PART
aimin 2 pleaze, keepin ♥
IT Real! Whatz Da Deal
        M OB

                    EARL
                — & —
            LETA

10 things I LOVE
about

    [L E]

10) He loves to just be him!!
9) His Courageousness
8) He's Down to Earth
7) His Body
6) His Confidence
5) His Mind
4) He Cuddles
3) He's Thoughtful
2) He's Generous
1) He's Amazing

08-31-08

"To: Little Earl"

Grandma couldn't get no card
so, I'am makeing one of my own!
"Happy Birthday" 97 yrs old correct?!
    Well hears you a Present, I
don't have much, but I have enough
for U! And to share.

♡ - U!

"Grandma"
09-05-08
"aka: Bouney"

June 1, 2004

DEAR EARL

    I HOPE THIS LETTER FIND YOU
DOING WELL AND ENJOYING LIFE TO
THE FMOST. I JUST WANTED TO
TAANR YOU FOR THE CARD YOU
SENT. EVERYONE AERE IS DOING FINE
AND SAYS HELLO.

       LOVE YOU

       LITTLE MOTHER
       Esther H. Smith